AF796504

# MAKING SENSE

Bold Ideas for Humanity's Survival
Through Education

SHAHID AHMED

Copyright © 2020 by Shahid Ahmed

All rights reserved. No part of this book may be reproduced or used in any manner without the copyright owner's written permission except for the use of quotations in a book review. For more information, email shahid@dopeace.org.

Every effort has been made to trace all copyright holders. The publishers will be pleased to make good any omissions or rectify any mistakes brought to their attention at the earliest opportunity.

Book edited by Lois Tuffin, and Jordon Waterwash
Formatted by Pankaj Runthala
Cover designed by Motaleb Israt and Pakaj Runthala

First paperback edition December 2020

Jacket photograph copyright © 2020 by Shahid Ahmed

ISBN 978-1-7338547-4-0

www.dopeace.org
You can contact the author at shahid@dopeace.org

**Disclaimer**

The events and conversations in this book have been portrayed correctly to the best of the author's memory. Some names and identifying details have been changed to protect the privacy of the people involved.

# Book Description

I have seen some clarity since writing the book *Under the Starry Nights: Low-cost Education to Thousands of Children in Slums*. There is a shot at clarity by passionately doing things in the pursuit of solutions. I have been working to educate children for the last six years in the slums of Bangladesh. There is a different perspective if you stand in the middle of a slum and look around. You ask why, and your mind takes you in all directions. I saw a connected world, and there was a domino effect. One leads to another, inevitably. The reverberation is felt everywhere in the world.

One example is the novel coronavirus. One person got it in Wuhan, China, and it has impacted every family in the world.

Why are many nations in conflict with each other? Why are there sharp divisions within countries? Why are we in the middle of deep ideological wars and moral confusion? We can say that some of these are nothing new, and we have seen them for the last several millennia. However, we are seeing a tipping point in its ferocity and a capability to produce enduring harm.

To dig into the reasons for this, I go back into history and discuss how the human brain was hardwired over thousands of years of evolution to be defensive and fearful about the next meal. We act on this fear individually: when we are poor, and when we are rich. This is when the filthy rich will continue to accumulate money, sometimes by breaking laws, even when he has far more than he can consume.

I looked into history to see how barbaric human beings have been and continue to be, as well as the heroic deeds we have performed and continue to perform with significant risk for the well-being of others. We could be extremely self-centered and overwhelmingly generous. The problem is that we are unpredictable, and one reckless act can hang humanity in the balance because we have developed such technology and continue to do so. Further, we have long started the cycle of destroying the very delicate environmental balance in our greed and unstoppable consumption. We have created mega multinational conglomerates too big to fail that have been dominating all aspects of the lives of all people.

The result is that the world has created inequities that are unprecedented. Eighty percent of the world population can be classified as poor, and are dominated by 20 percent of elites, who are better educated and more powerful, and who create policies to rig the playing field in their favor. The rich need cheap labor, and the lower class provides that. This 80 percent are subjected to human rights abuses in broad daylight. This is true, regardless of the system of government, ideology, and culture.

I have come to understand that only one thing can level the playing field, and that is education. All citizens of the world should be given the opportunity to acquire the equivalent of a bachelor's degree. This will increase the collective consciousness of the world. There is a better chance that citizens of the world will come together to make better choices to save humanity from its impending destruction. They will realize that we are all in it together, and if the ship called Earth sinks, we would meet the same fate, as we have nowhere else to go.

I argue that poor countries are poor because they have not provided primary school education to an overwhelming number of their children. The adult population's average education in developing countries is from second to sixth grade [1]. If they increase the average education up to eighth and tenth, then they will not be poor in the long run.

Finally, I provide a model by extrapolating data from my work in the slums of Bangladesh. This is for the poor nations to increase the level of education to beat poverty in 10 to 15 years. This is the lowest cost model, already proven to provide primary school education to 60,000 enrolled students, and can be ramped up within a short period of one to two years.

# Contents

To my wife Naheed

# Prologue

The novel coronavirus hit us like a tsunami after I had written about three-fourths of this book. The pandemic is still going full force without definite containment. The virus, called severe acute respiratory syndrome coronavirus 2 (SARS-Cov-2,), causes the coronavirus disease (COVID-19), which has already killed a million people globally, and is on its way to kill much more, before the only true defense, an effective vaccine, is in place. 'Oxfam's Interim Executive Chema Vera said:

> COVID-19 is the last straw for millions of people already struggling with the impacts of conflict, climate change, inequality and a broken food system that has impoverished millions of food producers and workers. Meanwhile, those at the top are continuing to make a profit: eight of the biggest food and drink companies paid out over $18 billion to shareholders since January even as the pandemic was spreading across the globe - ten times more than the UN says is needed to stop people going hungry. [2]

Meanwhile, the ten extreme hunger hotspots as per Oxfam are Yemen, Democratic Republic of Congo, Afghanistan, Venezuela, the West African Sahel, Ethiopia, Sudan, South Sudan, Syria, and Haiti.

In this book, I have discussed various scenarios of the new coronavirus and its impact on the poor and middle-income nations. I have a whole chapter devoted to our role in inviting or curbing the current and future pandemic.

# Introduction

The world is quite chaotic and arguably in a downward spiral to doomsday unless we all understand the interconnected factors involved and work systematically on the corrections needed by priority. The impending catastrophe due to escalating environmental degradation and the threat of annihilation due to nuclear war is always front and center. We have ended up here by a series of misguided actions over many generations, by allowing decisions to be made by a handful of mostly self-centered people who preferred personal interests over those of the community and humankind.

It all stems from the conflict of individual needs versus community interest. Individuals are programmed to control other individuals to satisfy their physical and psychological needs. Millions of years of evolution have hard-wired the brain to act on any real or perceived threat. Most threats are not real but perceived, yet the brain does not distinguish between the two and acts similarly in both cases. The human brain is always scanning for a threat and wants to respond to it for self-preservation. For the human brain, the world is a zero-sum game, meaning that the resources are finite: if someone else has it, then I do not. This includes material and non-material things.

Basic physical needs are food, clothes, and shelter for survival—a minimal amount will provide subsistence. To belong to a community is a basic psychological need. The most natural is belonging to a nuclear family of husband, wife, and children. However, the basic physical and psychological needs do not stop at subsistence once that is satisfied.

I believe that the brain has major difficulty understanding when the threat of deficient physical needs of food, clothes, and shelter is over. We keep eating food far more than the body requires. We buy clothes far more than required. We seek square footage of shelter far more than necessary. This deficiency of our brain of stopping when the physical needs are over has caused humankind unfathomable miseries.

The basic psychological need for belonging begins with the child's need for the mother. The child then learns to belong to the nuclear family, the tribe, and the sect. The belonging never stops, such as association with a group, the land, and language. An extension of the psychological need is the association with the belief system, particularly to which a child is exposed when growing up.

The psychological need is as strong as the physical need, and sometimes it is even stronger. Thus, the pursuit of craving for the longing for a belief system can lead to overcompensation, even to the extent of harming other communities to which they do not belong. This happens as the brain conceives any conflicting beliefs as a threat to their belongings, as cognitive dissonance [3].

Suppose the mind perceives that living is a zero-sum game and considers one person's winning as another person's loss, in relation to the physical and psychological needs. In that case, the world will live in a state of perpetual conflict. And, indeed, it is.

If the individuals in the world are caught in a zero-sum game, as they are destined by millions of years of evolution, then the Earth is programmed to be doomed from the get-go, and it is a matter of time when they are caught up with the ever-present crunch of the downward spiral.

Let us look at the individual actions that bring global consequences. An individual with a daily hustle meets physical needs. The brain does not know when physical acquisitions are sufficient. He or she continues seeking more, always fighting to get his or her share in this perceived dog-eat-dog world, and tends to overestimate. Some do become quite rich, yet the brain seeks more as the threat is not lifted. Rich become richer at the expense of the poor becoming poorer, as the rich could rig the rules of the games in their favor, which works against the poor getting the opportunity to get ahead.

This has created a world of haves and have nots. The class system was created since the beginning of times—a richer class and a poorer class. Much struggle has taken place over thousands of years in many societies to tease out this injustice, including many introductions of political and social systems, but to little progress. The two classes persist in all parts of the world.

The need for belonging drives an individual to a community, tribe, or sect. The community is driven by the wealthy, dominating individuals who are able to rig the rules in their favor, exploiting the rest for individual gains. The psychological need for belonging is thus used as a weapon to subjugate the rest for the gains of a few in the setup of a zero-sum game.

A subset of the need for belonging is recognition by the community for leadership roles, which includes awards and titles. Individuals are strongly driven by recognition as another zero-sum game. Only one individual can get the recognition and others lose.

If evolution has designed individuals to be on high alert for self-preservation, at the detriment of others, with cumulative results being the degradation of life on Earth, then there has to be intervention to stop this natural inclination. We should be willing to face this deficiency head-on.

## Rewiring the Brain

How do you upgrade a computer with glitches? Mostly by installing software that patches errors and improves performance.

How do you make humans less selfish, less harmful, and more caring for humanity? By rewiring the brain to make them more conscious of the long-term consequences. Note that I am not suggesting brainwashing to inculcate certain doctrines or dogmata of your choice. That will be, and has been, far more dangerous. I am suggesting making the brain more aware of real personal needs and how to balance the sense of belonging. As a result, people will not go way overboard and take all possible actions to deprive others of even making a decent living.

I am suggesting rewiring the brain so the need for belonging, recognition, display of success, and self-aggrandizing is not so senseless as to be harmful to the community and to humanity.

We need to fundamentally change how we prioritize our desire to live a life of well-being for ourselves and for others. Does our success necessarily mean that someone else must be unsuccessful? Does our desire of acquiring wealth mean that we need to rig the playing field for someone else to be poor?

Do we need to degrade the environment to achieve short-term gain at the expense of long-term disaster? Do we need to dispose of, for example, an unlimited amount of plastic that is severely endangering marine as well as human lives?

Do we need to spend a disproportionate amount of resources on war machines because of the fear of self-preservation, and spend that much less in the education of children, housing, and healthcare?

Rewiring the brain to assure ourselves we are not living in that much of a constant threat is the fundamental uphill battle humans have faced from the very beginning. This may have been true for thousands of years for the hunter-gathers, but it is no longer true in the current age.

Aggressive education on the meaning of a satisfactory life must be given by open debate and discussion. The satisfactory life is based on preconceived ideas developed from childhood by absorbing the norms of living all around us. Many of these ideas are flawed and harmful, but no such debate takes place earnestly when the child is growing up. They are simply accepted as true, without question.

## Reckless Consuming

Our brains play tricks on us. In fact, it is supposed to and has been wired over hundreds of thousands of years of evolution to hoard food and consume stuff. Hunter-gatherers lived through days of feast and famine. When lucky, they caught an animal that would provide plenty of food for the tribe. Then, they would go hungry for days until the next catch. The brain has not changed from this time, and acts the same even though we are not hunter-gatherers anymore. The result is that when food is presented to us, we eat voraciously. The problem is that there is no famine on a regular basis in most lives anymore. Thus we consume way over the required amount.

I believe the same applies to all other consumptions. Larger homes, more clothes, better cars, and more gadgets are extensions of hoarding dictated by the brain.

Let us look at the implications of excessive consumption. Every child born will require, theoretically, a home, a car, a fridge, lots of clothes, and lots of food over the years, among many other things. Over a lifetime this child will use huge amounts of electricity, heat, and other forms of energy for sustenance and entertainment. The definition of success will only drive the child to have bigger homes, better cars, more clothes, and more gadgets.

The increased consumption means bigger demands for more products, requiring more factories, providing more jobs, so the workers will have more disposable income to buy more of the stuff produced. Similar is the case for the service economy. With more jobs and income, people will use more of the services in healthcare, cosmetics, hair salons, fitness centers, and many other services.

A consumer society is dependent on the disposable income of people who are tied to jobs. Less disposable income will mean a slowing down of the economy and less production of goods and services. However, we have seen that the trend is more consumption over the years, stock rising consistently, and more wealth created [4].

If the whole system is based on insatiable consumption and is necessarily the consumption of natural resources, it results in the degradation of the environment that sustains us. Soon, we will hit the end of the rainbow, and the whole system will come to a screeching halt, or worse.

## The Vicious Cycle

We eat fast food because we are too busy producing to achieve success or making ends meet. We get sick by eating too much or eating unhealthy fast food. We go to the doctors, so they get work due to our bad eating practices. This makes the fast-food stores thrive and the doctors and hospitals make money at the peril of the consumer—this is not done so intentionally. The doctors have the incentive to increase revenue for the practice or the hospitals, so they order more tests and procedures. The increased cost of tests and procedures are paid for by the private insurance companies or Medicare, funded by taxpayers. This increases the health insurance cost to businesses or taxpayers.

What is the real cost of those fast-food hamburgers, fries, and soda? I might have paid only $6, but the real cost may be much higher— $50, $100, or $1,000? I may be way off, but I am trying to make a point, and the true cost is not so inconceivable.

We use electricity for almost everything. Energy is required to produce electricity. I may leave a light on just by neglect as the incremental cost is negligible. If billions of people do that, it will amount to significant energy waste. The electricity is provided using non-renewable energy sources, thus depleting them [5]. Worse, carbon dioxide is emitted to the atmosphere from the coal-fired plants, increasing the toxic particulates that we breathe, so we get sick [6]. Additionally, the Earth's temperature rises ever so slightly due to the greenhouse effect, melting the polar ice caps that increase the sea level. The rising water level submerges the lowlands displacing the population living there and damaging crops. Do not forget the particulates that make me sick, so I see the doctor and the healthcare industry can sustain its practices. . .

### What Is the Cost of My Innocuous Use of Plastic Bags?

Today, I used plastic bags when I picked up the groceries instead of asking for the paper bags they offered. I threw the plastic bags in the recycled dumpster and they were eventually disposed of. Somehow, they ended up in our water system or the sea. The microparticles we may consume by eating fish or by other means that makes me sick. In the meantime, islands of plastics in enormous quantities are floating in the oceans. The plastic water bottles are even found on the floors of the deepest oceans.

## What Is the Real Cost of the Bigger Home?

I bought a bigger home than I really need, as a big home will give me more space and the prestige of a successful man. A bigger home means more use of wood, so more trees will be cut somewhere. Fewer trees mean less oxygen that trees emit and more carbon dioxide that they neutralize. Thus, the carbon dioxide level in the atmosphere will increase, and the greenhouse effect will increase Earth's temperature, resulting in the consequences I talked about before.

## Prevention vs. Fix

It is surprising that many become physicians without taking a single course in nutrition. The medical profession does not indulge in much preventive advice per my observation, but relies on medicine, per their training. Perhaps because there is no money to be made through prevention; after all, the healthcare industry makes money when people become sick, not when they are healthy. I do not mean that doctors have any malicious intent to unnecessarily prescribe medicine or perform procedures. It is simply that the healthcare industry has no built-in incentive for preventive care. It is quite evident that preventive care using proper diet and exercise can keep people healthier for a longer period, saving—perhaps dramatically—the cost to the healthcare system.

What is the cost of the lost opportunity of reducing healthcare costs by providing preventive care using diet and exercise, so people do not get sick in the first place? I would say tremendous in both cost savings and the quality of life.

## Progress vs. Retrenchment

It is quite intuitive that there is no going back to simpler lives or reigning in technological progress. Arguably, those might have been the good old days, but now we have more knowledge, more awareness, and more appreciation about our place in this world and in the universe. We are finding the ever-evolving laws of physics at the microscopic level and honing into the deeper knowledge of how the universe was created and how it works. We have made significant progress in the understanding of biology and gene manipulation to impact healthcare. They are all good.

We erect skyscrapers, build megacities, and move the population from rural to urban areas. Businesses are generally booming, and wealth is being created at a faster pace.

Progress moves at the speed of a bullet train, but no one planned on that. It is going in whichever direction. Like pills that control disease, there are side effects to progress, and sometimes medications interact for the worse.

Building megacities consumes huge amounts of resources, causing the side effects of environmental damage, which sometimes causes newer health problems. These ailments require more research and innovation to create more pills that have different side effects. So, we are caught in a vicious feed with much more effort to keep the quality of life.

With an exponentially rising Earth's population, and with the growing consumption per person, it will not take too long when the demand will far exceed the production. New diseases will outpace the research for the cure, and discontentment will escalate causing increasing turmoil.

The problem is that the world is more and more mimicking a zero-sum game. For someone to win, someone else must lose, and that is a recipe for increasing conflict.

## The Zero-Sum Game

Let us assume that in an economic system there is only one person. She must take care of her own needs. She arranges for her own food, clothes, and shelter. This is awfully difficult as there is no one to share the work.

Let us add another person to the system. He arranges for food and shelter, while she cooks, cleans, and keeps the house tidy. It is now a little easier and the burden is shared. Add another person to take care of the shelter. With three people, we have the three tasks divided neatly, and they live happily. The basic requirements of life are taken care of. They need entertainment so they added a fourth person who can sing.

The two couples started producing children. They added a doctor to take care of their health, and a priest to protect them from harm by unknown and unexplained phenomena.

If their needs are met, exactly equally, everything is good. The rule is that one person makes shelter for all, one arranges for food, another cooks, the musician entertains, the doctor takes care of the health, and the priest protects.

As the population grows, expertise is divided, and if they share the workload equally, there is no problem. However, the problem comes when the productivity of an individual is lower; for example, if the singer fails to entertain, even when he is getting all the services from others. One way to keep the singer motivated is by penalizing him—by giving him fewer amenities as he is giving fewer services.

The other area of discord will occur when one person wants more share of services than others. If I want more clothes to wear than my share, then someone else will have fewer clothes as clothes are being produced equally for each person in this economic system.

This is a zero-sum game in which there are winners and losers. If the economic system is set up predominantly in this format, then we are forcing a class system, as some people will have more at the expense of others. The ones who acquire more would be tempted to win even more, as more wealth will allow them to rig the game in their favor. A zero-sum game is the product of greed in the face of limited resources. It is also cruel, as people with higher skills and influence will take advantage of those with lesser skills and influence.

There is another approach, where the economic system is based on needs, as opposed to the "winner takes all" model.

## The Need-Based Game

Each human being has the basic needs of food, shelter, and clothing. Beyond that, we need entertainment, which is everything else: art, sports, and leisure. In this economic system, resources are generated to ensure that the basic needs of each human being are ensured—no one will go hungry, be homeless, or without clothing.

The entertainment part of our needs is interesting and varied, and it is debatable as to how much of them are necessary. It may be crude to throw all needs beyond the basic needs into entertainment, but it makes the argument simple and on track. Animals, for example, mostly live and die on food and shelter (nature provides the clothes), with much less entertainment. But humans have evolved differently, which makes the discussion of the economic system relevant. The main difference is that humans have acquired bigger brains with built-in curiosity. In addition to innovation and discovery, humans have come to seek comfort with increasing intensity as they acquire the means to afford it.

How much does an individual need? Does a person need to be the king of the world—which is simply power over everyone else? One answer is yes, if he can; otherwise, he would like to control as many as he can. That is the guiding principle of human beings. A king would control his subjects; parents would control their children; the owner of a business would control her employees; priests would control their disciple; politicians would control the voting public; and the military would control the enemy or its own people.

I will contend that all needs that do not involve controlling others may be considered worthy of pursuing. This seems innocuous, but what about the needs that are purely perceived as pleasurable but do not involve controlling anyone else, such as living in multimillion-dollar homes, driving awfully expensive cars, and maintaining a luxurious lifestyle? I will argue that such a lifestyle cannot be acquired without controlling others, that is, without taking advantage of others in the zero-sum game.

If the economy is need-based, then it is equitable, as opposed to the zero-sum game. But is the equitable economy constrained and opposed to free-will? Should I be allowed to control as much I can muster, and any less will stifle my innovation, productivity, and curiosity? Will this disallow me to dream big and achieve success? This is strongly pegged to our perception of success—the one thing we are all trying to achieve.

## Reflecting on My Life

There are various moments that provide the opportunity to reflect on one's life, and the birthday is one. Socrates chose death, affirming that an unexamined life is not worth living. The question "Why am I here?" is perhaps rationally unanswerable.

But we are here, and what we are going to do with that fact is a reasonable question.

Everything emanates from core values. Everyone has them, whether we consciously reflect on them or not. If all decisions are reflective of our core values, then it is worth examining exactly what they are. Without such an examination, we are perhaps slaves to our core values.

Where do we get our core values? I surmise that we get them from our role models—our parents first, then extended family and friends we grow up near. Our teachers at an early age can also have a lot of influence on us. For example, if a child observes his or her parents lying, then that is what will go into the stack of core values, not what the parents tell their children, as children soak the values by observation.

It all depends on what the child observes to be true when growing up, then it is quite unchangeable, without significant intervention. This is what I have seen in 70 years of my life. That is why I have embarked upon educating children from the very beginning and providing an environment that provides ethical values—truth, honestly, compassion, respect, justice, and giving—as our children are the recipient of such values themselves. Our teachers at DoPeace inculcate these values into the students, and we believe that this is something that will remain with them.

My father died in his mid-40s but growing up I frequently noticed honesty and respect for others as his core values. He refused to accept bribery, something that was not far from the norm in his community of high-ranking government officials. Human values superseded religious reprimands in his books. He was an open-minded, liberal-leaning, and well-read individual. I believe I followed quite a bit from him, internally, without making much effort. I remember that I would never accept charity from family and friends when we were having trouble for a period after my father's death.

I grew up mostly in Dhaka, Bangladesh, and lived in Karachi, Pakistan, for about five years. It will be hard for an American to understand my experience growing up in a poor nation, where the rules of the social norm are quite different. When I arrived at Iowa State University in 1976 and started my graduate studies, I surely had a crash course in American culture, which appeared quite strange and different. I would say that it took me several years before I found myself reasonably adjusted in the United States of America.

I am far from perfect, but the moral compass I obtained in my early childhood has remained with me. My family still accuses me of not giving my children the strong religious teachings of Islamic culture. I must admit that I was never very adamant on religion myself, something I might have picked up from my father. However, my two brothers and two sisters are quite religiously inclined, so my father did not have the same influence on everyone.

As you can see in this book, my advocacy for the equality of human beings, no matter where they come from or what circumstances they have inherited, is of primary importance to me. This supersedes all other conditions and affiliation.

# Success

The criteria for success are the greatest drivers in an individual's life. Life's activities depend on what is embedded as the perceived goals set in the mind either explicitly or implicitly. Goal setting is historically an exercise of self-achievement in competition with peers. If I set a goal to be the CEO or the manager of a company, then that means I will be beating other competitors who may be setting the same goals. The other types of goals are those that not only benefit individuals but also lifts the community.

Goal setting is such a powerful tool that those who set out to properly embed the goal in mind have a much higher likelihood of achieving it, as opposed to those who do not explicitly set up any goals or do not do it properly.

## Satisfaction as a Better Measure of Success

I have discussed the flaws of how success is measured by the riches you have, and how this has created one of the most misguided goals people have. I would change the measure of success to how satisfied you are with your life. Although it is obvious that a poor person who cannot get the necessities of life will be unsatisfied; however, being super-rich does not guarantee a satisfying life either. Life's satisfaction stems from a purposeful life, in addition to having a threshold of money for the basic needs of food, clothes, and shelter. Research has indicated that any wealth beyond a threshold does not add proportionally to the joy in life. Therefore, working hard to accumulate more money beyond this threshold may become counterproductive to our well-being.

Satisfaction in life can be different for different people, and money is only one factor. Others can be education, family, friends, and entertainment. If you sacrifice all your time for money, then you can lose out on other items, and success could be elusive. For example, in the USA, making more than $60,000 to $75,000 per year does not bring a proportional amount of happiness.

Let us say I accumulated several million dollars, sacrificing family life. I would live a comfortable life, but it would be overkill. The incremental comfort I gain with additional money would be marginal. In addition, I may not be gaining on the total satisfaction score.

For example, let us say that life's satisfaction is measured by five factors: money, family, friends, health, and your values such as the preservation of human rights. Also, for the sake of this discussion, let us give equal weight to each of these five factors. That is, if we are prudent and lucky, we will divide our time such that we achieve 20 percentage points of satisfaction on each of the five items, and you get the maximum satisfaction of 100 percent.

If we spent lopsided time in the pursuit of money and did make a lot of money, but, say, only scored 10 percent in the four other four items. The satisfaction gained for making money is 20 percent, but the total on all the others is 40 percent (10x4), thus the total comes down to 60 percent, a significantly lower satisfaction number.

Thus, considering true satisfaction is multidimensional and that we need to be well rounded in all items, our perspective in life will be different.

Imagine you are dying with lots of money, but lonely without family or friends. Would you be satisfied with all the money in the bank, but have nothing more? The truth is you will be leaving your wealth here for someone else to benefit from. What good is it to you?

If you agree that satisfaction is a better measure of success, then the whole outlook on life changes quite dramatically. Suddenly other factors such as family, friends, health, and the well-being of the community become more important. Any decisions related to your life and career will not be guided solely by the money you earn.

We know that your decisions impact your household, the extended family, and the community in which you interact. Further, there is an impact, however small it may be, on the nation and the world. As people strive to be successful, it is simply not by building wealth. It is also building other factors that satisfy a human being, which may be different for different people. For a well-rounded individual, it will always include factors that will build a just and thriving community for all. This way we will be deviating from the wealth-building as the sole success criteria, which border on the zero-sum game. As discussed before, a zero-sum game is when you win, but others lose. I believe that a significant number of conflicts in this world arise as we have made success as a zero-sum game.

With nations built on satisfaction as the success criteria, I believe there will be much more humane societies based on trust built among all. The conflict among China, Russia, and the USA is based on a severe lack of trust, resulting in fear for security. This fear has resulted in so much waste of resources on military buildup and warmongering that is simply a huge waste of money. Even though more than 75 years have passed since any world war, we are constantly involved in smaller warfare for various political and ideological reasons. The grief of humanity has been perpetual, with a relentless pursuit of dominance.

## Social Impact vs. Fame

I have heard a lot about the curse of being famous, or worse, being rich and famous. I have experienced neither of them, but any suspicion of losing my freedom is quite alarming to me. I can simply imagine the horror of walking the streets while being noticed by the people around me, or worse, approaching me for a handshake, a conversation, or an autograph simply to touch a celebrity. I have immense sympathy for those famous people or celebrities, as I do not want to be under the watchful eyes of the public, paparazzi, or journalists.

I am quite sure that there are people who would crave to be famous or a celebrity, just for the heck of it, as this may give them a kick to their living. Perhaps a need to be superior or an elite is at the core of this. The attention of a lot of people surrounding you can be intoxicating. An adoring crowd can stroke your ego like nothing else.

Famous people or celebrities perhaps feel power over others, as they are showered with adulation and love. The pleasure of having power over anyone has a well-known effect on the human psyche as power provides an impulse to manipulate. It also requires a strong ethical footing to resist the temptation to manipulate, and it is best that such power is checked so the temptation is not easily materialized.

Does success equate to fame? That depends on the definition of success, as I have discussed before. People who perpetuate their success by being well known or famous, such as an actor, or a model, must maintain their fame at whatever cost. However, fame could be an unintended consequence of someone dedicated to social good like a writer, a painter, or a singer.

It has come late in my life, but it is quite clear to me that the dots of cause and effect must be connected as a starting point to halt the downward spiral of human decline on Earth. One thing affects the other, then it can have a domino effect, and that effect can gain unstoppable momentum until all the pieces crumble. It starts by looking at all the activities with the lenses of social good. Does that activity harm the Earth or help it?

If the mission of social good is not to pursue fame, the impact of such a mission is delivered quite powerfully. In opposition to that, if the intent is to gain fame or personal benefits, the impact of the mission is diluted, and it does become ineffectual in the long run.

The definition of my success does not include being famous, but I have also not accomplished social good to the extent that would attract any big attention, so, by default, I don't need to worry about something that is not going to happen anyway.

## Conflict Resolution by the Force of Love

I have this wild theory that has been sitting on my mind for many decades. It sounded so silly that I never seriously discussed it with anyone. It is love as the driving force to resolve conflict.

Let us take one of the enduring conflicts in the world, the Arab-Israeli conflict. Let us imagine that one million Israeli men, women, and children decided to march across the border with gifts into the Palestinian territory. As they startle the Palestinians, they hug the men, women, and children, as they offer their love and affection. They promise they will not leave any stone unturned to make sure the lives of Palestinians will improve. They will build schools for children, train the younger generation skills to be employed, and make sure that the human rights of the Palestinians are improved. They do this unconditionally, with no strings attached.

If the above scenario is possible, what will this do? It will shake up the Palestinian belief that Israelis do not care. That they are simply there for the land grab, and will try everything to hold on to it. Even honest gestures to resolve issues are taken as ploys to continue the stronghold. The mindset of the Palestinians will be shaken, and they will see a glimpse of humanity in the Israeli families.  Currently, they have truly little interaction with them and mostly see the armed Israeli guards.

Take the case of the conflict in Kashmir. Pakistan and India have fought three wars over this region. The first thing that Indians can do is overwhelm the Kashmiris through a love march of thousands of men, women, and children, showering their well wishes and gifts. Imagine the awe and mental jolt they would face. It would shake the negative belief that the Kashmiris have about India, even when it is quite evident that most Indians are well-wishers and absolutely do not hate Kashmiris. It is time that most Indians take charge of the destiny of the Indian subcontinent and take active measures to bring peace to the region.

Consider the case of the centuries-old conflict between Black and White people in the USA. The injustice and inhumane treatment of Black people is very well known and is ever-present. Just look at the proportion of Black people who are incarcerated or murdered year after year. Yet, nothing concrete is done to alleviate the continuous hurt that is ever-present among Black people. What if the White citizens get up in thousands and storm Black neighborhoods to visibly show solidarity and love to them? This will shake up their deep belief that White people are not their well-wishers, or worse—that they hate them.

The force of love can revolutionize the world. The very core of harmony in the world is possible because of this premise: It is hard for you to hate a person who loves you and is your well-wisher. This very fact can be capitalized at a much wider level. It is much easier to resolve a conflict with another individual if it is established that you do not want to hurt the other person and want the other person to thrive. The solutions are then win-win, and both parties will be much more willing to be flexible for a resolution. Absent the trust, there is hardly any enduring resolution. Trust is the most important ingredient of any meaningful relationship.

## Happiness as the New Currency

This is a little repetitive, but this concept is worth looking from a slightly different angle. Imagine the currency of wealth is happiness, and we can measure how much of this currency each of us has. This is quite different from wealth measured by, for example, US dollars, or euros, or Bangladesh taka. Although it is obvious a poor person who cannot get the necessities of life will be poor by any measure, super-rich is not guaranteed to be so rich when measured with the new currency.

The distribution of wealth can be easier to spread equitably when we can adopt the new currency, as happiness level will soon flatten for all after acquiring a threshold of material wealth. It also impacts the bragging rights of individuals as there are other factors that determine wealth. Material acquisition of fame and fortune can translate into the new currency only marginally.

Happiness as a currency will be a great equalizer, as many without having wealth beyond the basic threshold will be called super-rich in the new currency. This is not necessarily because such people are lazy, uneducated, or incapable of collecting the material wealth, but because their priorities are different. People who live a wholesome life get more currency. Happiness stems generally from a well-rounded life, and particularly from meaningful relationships—anyone completely devoid of that, on one extreme, will be quite poor. On the other extreme, as pointed out above, a person who cannot make ends meet is also quite poor. When measured in the new currency, both are equally poor.

The instant social status bestowed by all cultures to people with material wealth, and thus power, is one of the most destabilizing factors contributing to the inequities around the world. Because of this, many people will do anything they can get away with to acquire material wealth. Many will play the system, take advantage of cheap labor, manipulate people, take shortcuts, invent moral authority, impose favorable binding rules, and downright hurt others. The cultural worship of material wealth is universal, strong, and intoxicating. Many will be tempted to acquire, far more than they will ever be able to use, by blatantly breaking laws. All this stems from a flawed mental model that success is equal to material wealth and equal to happiness.

A culture that adopts the new model of currency will not reward the unwarranted accumulation of material wealth. Thus, the cut-throat culture of beating others to get ahead to acquire more profit will tone down. Mega businesses will be unpopular or unnecessary as the shareholders will indulge in acquiring currency in happiness more than maximizing profit. More small businesses will spring up as the playing field will not be as rigged. The standard of living of the general masses will rise.

Business operators will think more about the environment. People will think more of the general good, as happy people will be more willing to spread happiness. Happy citizens make a happy country. A happy country will be open to having a good relationship with another happy country. Trust will increase and spending on war enterprise will decrease. The threat to world peace will be jointly resolved, including threat due to disease and pandemic.

It all starts with one happy person. It is opposite to what we are facing now with COVID-19. One person got infected and now the whole world is affected. Make happiness your currency, and, similarly, the whole world will be infected with this happiness virus. It will change the world as never before.

## Sharing vs. Hoarding

It is well established that people essentially use a fraction of their possessions, yet they keep buying. For example, in the average American home, there are 300,000 items [7] but how many do they really use? In the current consumer society, shopping is an entrenched habit. On the days when malls are closed, many people are at a loss for to what to do. Buying has gone much beyond the necessity. In fact, the whole economy is tightly linked to consumer buying. Any slowdown in consumer buying is an ominous sign of slowing down of the economy—related to loss of jobs, and reduced investment in equipment and projects.

Excessive purchasing is seldom frowned upon. How many shirts, TVs, microwaves, and cars do we need? Do we buy it because it is a good deal or because we need it? In many instances, people will not hesitate to buy on credit if they do not have cash, even when they could get by without buying it. Without going into the financial well-being of being deeply in debt, let us look at the environmental impact of the manufacturing of goods, especially the carbon footprint. Manufacturing of any goods involves the emission of greenhouse gases. It is well known that these gases result in the warming of Earth, associated with deleterious effects on the environment. The glaciers are melting fast, and the expected rise of the water level is a real threat to many countries that are at or near sea level.

It is difficult to relate our compulsive buying habits with eventual environmental degradation, as the cause and effect are not immediately visible. However, there is no denying that the cumulative effect will be detrimental either soon, or in the distant future. However, if we substantially reduce collective buying, then it will slow down the economy, and result in job loss. Are we between a rock and a hard place, then?

Even though reckless buying on credit has economic consequences, the environmental impact is more related to the manufacturing process, especially the use of energy and its carbon footprint. The use of coal to generate electricity unavoidably results in the emission of large quantities of $CO_2$ and other harmful materials in the environment. On the other hand, the electricity generated by using renewable energy such as solar and wind has a negligible carbon footprint. The share of renewable energy as the source of electricity is currently negligible, leaving coal-fired plants as the main culprit. So, any manufacturing of consumer goods uses electricity and consequently results in pollution. This is true not only for consumer goods but also for any equipment or products made for business use.

## The Hunt for Happiness

It is said frequently that the goal of human life is to be happy. Paradise is stated to be a place of perpetual happiness. How to be happy has been explored incessantly. Having established that we need to do something that will attain our state of happiness, we continue to explore various avenues.

I have discussed the futility of considering wealth as the sole measure of success. But all of us who have health issues know that vibrant health is a major contributor to happiness. A sound mental and physical health provides the backbone for a quality of living, and the absence of this sucks the air out of happiness. It is, therefore, extremely important that one needs to be diligent to be up-to-date on information leading to better health since such information is ever-changing and fraught with confusion. Correct judgment is necessary for the application of healthy living habits and we must be ready to modify those habits as new information becomes available.

Relationship building is another crucial factor for happiness. Humans have evolved to be social beings, living in groups and communes from the very beginning for survival. The need to interact with each other socially is hard-wired in the brain by necessity. We find consolation in sharing problems and feel joy in sharing happiness. We interact to innovate, teach each other knowledge and skills, and band together to ward off threats. The skills to build and sustain good relationships, and forgo the toxic ones are perhaps the key to happy living.

In my earlier life, my mindset was to become rich so I could have everything I wanted. However, I found quite a bit of resistance and conflict with my very nature. I went to The Wharton School of Business in their Executive MBA Program, which was quite a learning experience. It was essentially about the theory and skills for wealth building. Among our cohort of about 80 students, all had managerial positions at various companies. We were rather young professionals driven to succeed and go up the ladder in our respective corporations. We wanted to be rich and make a name for ourselves.

I had a revulsion to the concept of being super wealthy and that has stuck with me to this day. I believed that anything beyond being comfortable should be given away for the greater good. I had a dislike for impressing others with displays of wealth, such as super big homes, expensive watches, and over the top cars. I never had the desire to compete with anyone in accumulating wealth.

Those who have wealth-building as the main criterion for success will have a difficult time being happy, as they will always lag behind those who have more wealth. The road to more wealth, not necessarily for adequate comfort but as a measurement of success, is a slippery slope fraught with trouble and leads to the feeling of perpetual inadequacy with what they already have. Also, wealth as a metric is not entirely in our control, and today's wealthy may be tomorrow's less wealthy, to no fault of their own.

I believe that the definition of success must include the pursuit of something bigger than self, which necessarily relates to the well-being of others. I trust that the human brain has an evolutionary component of this, even when I do not have concrete scientific evidence of it. My personal experience points me to such a conclusion.

A major factor that leads to happiness is love for others. Absent love, life is barren and happiness elusive. Any encounter with another individual must have love as an underlying basis. Only then we can encounter happiness on a regular basis. Love is a basic and a natural instinct of life, while hate is cultivated. On the flipside, anyone who encounters another life with hate will bring unhappiness on a regular basis.

I have concluded that the main purpose of life is to love and be loved. The rest may be necessary, but not sufficient. This purpose is the sole reason why our world will be peaceful, and humans will survive on the planet.

I believe that happiness is only achieved vicariously. You feel happy when you make another individual happy. You do not achieve enduring happiness directly, for example, by stuffing your life with expensive items. That is why being part of something bigger than yourself and approaching any encounter with others with love brings happiness to you. That is why a person is unhappy with the degree to which he or she is selfish. Thus, a purely selfish person will have no enduring happiness. Conversely, by extrapolation, a completely selfless person will have the utmost happiness in the long run, even when it is idealistic, and I do not know if a person can be completely free from selfish desires.

## Reworking the Definition of Success

If the current definition of success is misguided and may ultimately lead to catastrophic results, then how should this be framed in a way that aligns with human needs? But, first, why do we have this compulsion to succeed? I believe this is because we have this competitive streak, immense curiosity, and the need for a significant and perpetual challenge for the satisfaction of making life worthwhile. Edmund Hillary said that he conquered Mount Everest because it was there. This may defy any logic for some, but that does sum up human nature to overcome incredible odds and do what may seem to be impossible now.

The main challenge is to change from confrontation to collaboration. The problem is that confrontation seems to be more tantalizing than collaboration, and the human brain understands that raw instinct quite well. All sports and the huge number of spectators feed on that instinct. There are no popular physical sports where two teams collaborate to achieve a certain challenge—as that will be hardly thrilling.

However counter-intuitive it may seem, the collaboration-based success criteria at the individual, national, and international level may be the only way to save the world from its misery.

As the name indicates, collaboration-based goals are set by two or more collaborators to achieve a goal and has two components: (1) Create a joint goal, and (2) Make sure that both or all succeed. I am not talking about collaboration as a joint venture or partnership. I am talking about producing products of the same functionality and for the same market, but the product is differentiated for market segments. In the current market environment, they will be competitors, but for our model, they will collaborate, not to price fix, but to make sure they all have a good shot at succeeding. Collaboration does not mean that the trade secrets are revealed, or the operational techniques are given away. But it does mean that companies home in on the specialization for a niche. The mega conglomerates dominating consumers worldwide must relinquish their power, giving way to small businesses that specialize.

Collaborative-based models simply mean that one company does not become monolithic, dominant, and too big to break.

Currently, large companies simply bankrupt or devour smaller companies, causing a lot of harm to the social fabric of society. Mega businesses have too much power over the workers and the clients, and for all practical purposes, they have the power to violate democratic values, human rights, personal privacy, and environmental sustainability. Large companies make hierarchies among people, mostly based on income. They create a few billionaires and millionaires, but the overwhelming majority are poor workers who may not earn living wages, all under the umbrella of the same company.

First, I contend that the world does not need billionaires, some of them having wealth equal to an entire country or more. Collaboration based business environments will make sure that a huge number of small businesses will succeed, without the highly skewed and lopsided concentration of wealth.

The definition of success must be scaled and redirected towards the long term benefit of society, without the motivation of the "winner takes all" mentality that exploits all possible loopholes to dodge taxes, deceives with slick marketing and sales tactics, hides the weaknesses, and maximizes profits with questionable gimmicks. We have witnessed too many of them, all designed to concentrate wealth and power among only a few.

If happiness is one of the major goals of being successful, then the accumulation of wealth can help only to a certain extent. Beyond that, many other factors become relevant and money loses its importance, as discussed before. If that were the case, then why put such heavy emphasis on the accumulation of wealth? Why not have wealth up to a point that matters, and make sure that all others achieve the same success? Why design a society with haves and have-nots, with a highly skewed distribution of wealth that does not serve even the wealthy as they have no need for that?

It is high time that we think about the collaboration-based definition of success criteria that make individuals succeed to acquire necessary wealth through a business environment that helps all and not only a few.

## Beyond Self-Preservation

To work for survival is a built-in motivation, and that is the most primitive instinct for all living things. Humans have now progressed to the point where they need to work for only part of their living time. They can have other areas of interest that can preoccupy their free time.

What motivates us beyond the need to—what I call—primitive survival? We may have the option to do several things to survive. Out of them all, what motivates us to choose one or the other?

There is this two-tiered pursuit: one is to make a living, and another is totally different—to do what we genuinely like. When I am searching for a true motivation in life, it is the other pursuit that is more interesting. It is simplified and powerful when the two pursuits are merged into one. Then there is no confusion and the person hones onto a single goal. The motivation not only provides the primitive living but fulfills the inner desire to achieve the potential nature has gifted us.

The important point is that the true calling takes you beyond self-preservation. I have addressed in my previous discussions on how self-preservation has pushed us in a divergent, harmful path. I am arguing that a true calling, whatever it may be for an individual, is a uniting force. This contrasts with making the sole purpose of life self-preservation, which is turning out to be quite destructive for life on Earth.

## Beware of Distractions

Distractions are one of the biggest killers of our dreams. The norm is that the mind is racing in many different directions and has difficulty focusing on one thing for long. The inability to keep the mind quiet and letting it jump from one task to another, without finishing any, is one of the greatest causes of inefficiency, dissatisfaction, and anxiety.

This happens because of a fundamental flaw in our mental model. (I have addressed the mental model of living in my book, *Under the Starry Nights.*) Without our firm direction, the mind is unable to prioritize and thinks that all tasks are equally important. Therefore, the mind will pick up any task that arises at the moment, without regard to its importance.

We first need to determine the priority of the tasks to be accomplished; if not, then the default position is, as said above, that all tasks are equally important. So, the impulse is to do anything that pops up in your mind for some reason.

We need to take our time to plan the hourly, daily, monthly, yearly, and life goals. Without that, time will simply slip by, minute by minute, and you may accomplish nothing worthwhile over a lifetime.

So, stop now and determine what you ultimately want to accomplish. Anything that directly helps you achieve that goal is relevant, and all other things are distractions. Spend, say, 10 percent of your time planning before doing.

Stop selling your time to the highest bidder. Otherwise, you are not in control of your time, and the tasks you do are not yours but someone else's, and this will keep you dissatisfied. A good employer should make sure that they align their vision with the worker's inner values and goals—making the endeavor worthwhile for everyone.

I have articulated my vision in the DoPeace vision statement: *To enable children in the slums of the world to get sustainable and high-quality education at low cost while creating a strong partnership with the communities involved.*

Our staff of over 100 are chosen carefully, so they all are enthusiastic about this vision. This fulfills their inner values. They love to spend every minute of their time in this pursuit. The tasks they perform daily are their tasks and they are totally aligned with the organizational goals.

That is how we are a strong, coherent, and goal-seeking organization, determined to make a difference in the lives of disadvantaged and poor children. We do not allow ourselves to be distracted too often and we keep focused on what is critical.

## Hard Choices

As a nonprofit organization dealing with the education of slum children, DoPeace has taken performance issues seriously in our six years of work in Bangladesh and are close to mimicking the intensity of a for-profit organization. Inadequate education has a stark downside to it. Students will simply not be able to make it and drop out, or be unsuccessful in the long run.

We have determined that the only way students will be motivated to succeed is when they can perform at the upper level at primary school. This requires a relentless pursuit of quality teaching at DoPeace Learning Centers. Anything less than that will be a disservice to the students, their parents, and the community.

It has been a struggle for us to filter this idea into the psyche of all the stakeholders. It is easy to simply get into the act of school building and associate activities with success. I totally understand that it could be akin to building a house of cards that can disintegrate in the face of known or unknown challenges.

There is a perceived incoherence when associating slum education with quality. The children, the parents, and the community are ill-prepared to demand quality when something is provided free of cost. However, we should know that our mission will see an unsuccessful outcome, without producing long-term results, if we ignore quality.

We have put together daily, monthly, and yearly performance measures that are monitored closely. When the measures are not met consistently, perhaps over months and years, we have hard choices to make. We are in a better position to do so as we have a decentralized organization. We are not locked into one or two NGOs implementing our educational model, but seven in total. We have competitive pressure built into the system by making our monthly performance evaluations transparent to all. And we are willing to let go of the organizations that are consistently on the fringes of performance.

We are building a nonprofit organization with a competitive streak and are willing to make hard choices generally in the realm of a for-profit business. And this is all in the interest of high-quality education for the most disadvantaged and poor children.

# Education, Democracy, and Human Rights

Without a substantially educated populace, true democracy is not possible, and ubiquitous human rights cannot be delivered. Before I explain what I mean, I should define what I mean by a substantially educated person. Actually, it is easier to define who is not substantially educated—he is the one who has not made an effort to gather well-rounded information on the critical aspects of a decision that has a major impact on the current or future well-being of society. This is the person who may or may not have obtained a college education, but it is definitely helpful, even when the person can gather significant knowledge by experience or exposure to the vast amount of information available in this digital age.

A person with substantial information has a high likelihood of making an accurate decision, even though it is not guaranteed. However, it is far less likely to make accurate decisions by someone with scant information.

It is easier to exploit an uneducated or less informed individual who will take certain doctrines at face value. In a zero-sum game, which I have discussed before, personal gains are obtained by exploiting other individuals, which is possible by convincing them to relinquish or bestow power or wealth. In a society with a substantially uneducated or less informed population, this amounts to the propensity to exploit vast populations for the benefit of some.

Lack of education is the prime reason for the segregation of society into upper and lower classes based on wealth, education, and income. Further, this class distinction is maintained by the upper class by flexing their wealth to enforce policies that create further opportunities to strengthen their position, and at the same time, reduces the opportunities for the lower class. The result is that the upper class gains more wealth and power, while the lower class becomes poorer, with less say in determining their destiny.

A general rule is that democracy is stronger in societies with a higher proportion of education, while it is weaker in societies with lower proportions of education. Dictatorship, military rule, religiosity, autocracy, and demagoguery are staples of many uneducated societies.

If we assume that the lack of proper information or education is an impediment to accurate decision-making, then it can be argued that democracy would be a choice that may not benefit an uneducated society and might even harm the population. A case in point is the fascist regime of the Nazis Partly headed by Adolf Hitler who manipulated the German population to willingly relinquish their authority in favor of his dictatorship. That resulted in mass murder and unprecedented damage.

Ideally, true democracy is when the population is so educated as to be able to weigh in on all significant policies and decisions with a secure means that supports the polling at any instant. The Greeks implemented this successfully in the sixth century in the city-states, in which each citizen (only males though) had a direct vote as if they were elected representatives. In this simple but equitable system, all the middlemen (middle tier elected officials) are eliminated and the decisions are made directly by the citizens. The reasons for the middlemen and women are supposedly for expediency. The so-called experts who are more articulate and may or may not have superior knowledge are relegated to make rather complex decisions. Further, it is assumed that ordinary citizens have no time to investigate or participate in direct voting on critical issues, such as war and peace.

In the absence of direct democracy, the current approach is indirect democracy, where ordinary citizens elect middlemen or women, who in turn elect other middlemen or women who participate in the decision-making. There may be many layers of separation between the ordinary citizens and the decision-makers, and there are pros and cons to it. The pros are that ordinary, and perhaps incapable, citizens are relieved from the rather complex decisions that require accurate and more technical analysis of the long-term impact of the decisions. However, this is not the case if we assume that ordinary citizens are quite capable of making such decisions. The cons are that some of the incapable or corrupt representatives are selected, even if they do not have the state's well-being in mind. Rather, they act to achieve personal wealth or power, or both, by misleading those who elected them.

Of course, any kind of democracy that involves ordinary citizens is better than a country ruled outright by a dictator or demagogue, in which case the citizen does not participate in the decision-making in any substantial way. In this case, the liberty of the citizens is trampled, fear is widespread, and observing human rights is the least of the priorities of the state. A dictator basically uses the country's resources to subjugate the citizens, such as consolidating military might, funded by the citizens' money. Deluged with power, the dictator plays God with the citizens and is not subject to any restraints.

A fractured democracy also has the loophole to create dictators or autocracy. These institutions are the facades of democracy, and it mostly takes place in some of the developing countries or where society allows dictators in disguise. These countries have no compulsion to create or follow rules of law, and the powerful are immune to any boundaries that restrain them.

## The Ugly Side of Democracy

A republic governed by the representation of people has provided the best and proven governance to bestow coveted freedom. Still, it has managed to create an economic divide that has produced overwhelming grief to the masses. As I have pointed out before, 80 percent of the world's population is quite poor, making less, sometimes far less, than 10 US dollars per day. Just ponder a little on this reality. What kind of lifestyle is possible with this income? They cannot afford decent housing, food, or clothes, while other amenities taken for granted in advanced nations are practically nonexistent.

The world revolves around the upper 20 percent of the world's population, or much less. Others are relatively uneducated, ill-informed, unaware, and hardly able to participate in the decision-making that governs their lives. The fact is that they are irrelevant and invisible in the current democratic system.

If you look at democratic nations, the wealth divide is still striking. The world has produced super-rich people, so much so that the combined wealth of only eight people is more than the combined wealth of the lower half of the world population [8]. Per one conservative estimate, Bill Gates' wealth exceeds forty countries [9]. Several others are similarly rich. This is in the name of a free market, and without any significant tax burden; or worse yet, tax loopholes and tax havens have protected them from paying proportionate taxes.

If you are unfortunate and part of the lower 80 percent of the world's population, you likely cannot afford to buy this book. You will be represented by, comparatively, wealthy people, and many of them do not have any appreciation of how you live. Your representative will be too busy protecting their power and wealth first and catering to other wealthy individuals or corporations who will be in cahoots with them for mutual benefits. The actual protection of the poor and the disadvantaged are furthest from the minds of the representatives. This is the main reason that 80 percent of the world population is stuck at the lower rung of the ladder.

The rich and the poor live in two different worlds, in a parasitic relationship—the rich using the poor for cheap labor. The rich will make as much money as they can muster to rig policies and laws that will allow them to retain and grow their wealth. The democratic system allows the divide and perpetuates it, as the wealthy few essentially control all the power of decision-making.

If you are poor, it will be an uphill battle to rise significantly above the poverty line—Democracy will allow this to happen—but will not guarantee your well-being for a respectable life if you cannot make it. Democracy will, however, give an easy pass to those who have managed to acquire assets.

Democracy, in its current form, is humiliating to the poor and disadvantaged. The wealth distribution is very much unacceptable to any rational mind, as the rich continue to become richer, and the poor, poorer. The only reason this is possible is because the poor do not know how to stop this. They are quite unaware, uneducated, and unskilled to take charge, change laws, and stop the loopholes that allow the rich to exploit them. If history is any indication, it is quite evident that the rich will rein in and hold onto their power and not relent the wealth they have created on behalf of just distribution. The current form of the democratic institution will not help the poor much.

There is this setup of services to the poor and the disadvantaged by the wealthy: tax breaks for charity work; recognition of heroes who alleviate the suffering of the poor; giving prizes to workers who dedicate their lives for the well-being of the poor; and market-based innovations that will provide water, toilet, clothes, and shelter. The whole concept of the apparent generosity of the wealthy is upside-down. The minority of 20 percent or less is indulging in charity work for the majority of 80 percent or more. This seems odd. The well-being of the majority should be the norm, and if anything, charity work should be to the minority of the population in a democracy. I believe this moral dilemma has caused the super-rich to create a facade of humanitarian work to make them feel less guilty. The rich humanitarians get together and congratulate one another on their charitable work for humanity and live happily in their comfortable lives.

The point is that there should not be any humanitarian giving for the overwhelming majority of the world population. They should already be better off—with the right form of democracy that works for them.

The current system of democracy has allowed the inhumane distribution of wealth and has divided nations, societies, and individuals into extremely rich and extremely poor. That is possible only through exploitation, where the poor are used for cheap labor without any shame, under cover of laws that are rigged to protect such exploitation.

There is no justification or moral basis for delegating 80 to 90 percent of the world's population to hand to mouth daily struggle, so that 10 to 20 percent of the rest can enjoy the fruits of the labor of the poor. That imbalance arises from a rigged democratic system.

# Global Agenda

Is there a need for global goals resulting in equitable human rights, wealth, and freedom for the citizens of the world? Are we able to define what is equitable? These human values differ from country to country, and from various tribes within a country. Each independent country is considered sovereign, and interference in running any state is considered unallowable per the rules of the United Nations. A country can be run by a dictator who can blatantly and ruthlessly violate human rights and can still be an equal member of the UN with impunity. In 2017, 24,000 Rohingya were brutally murdered in Myanmar and one million were displaced to Bangladesh. This will go down as one of the worst hate crimes organized and perpetrated by a state. Yet, Myanmar remains a member of the UN without any repercussions and without any concrete steps taken against them.

Recent history is replete with human rights violations without significant consequences to the perpetrators. There is little recourse if the Security Council does not pass a resolution unanimously, and most resolutions are vetoed by one or more members of the Security Council. In a global environment that is quite divisive in the methods of running the state, a just approach to freedom to the citizens, living the daily lives, distribution of resources, and harmony among various tribes and factions is a daunting task.

The world's resources are finite, including land, freshwater, fossil fuel, and minerals—and these are mostly non-renewable. With the rapid increase of the world's population, there is intense competition to acquire the resources. This is a zero-sum game. The more I have, the less you will have, as the pie is finite. The more powerful you are, the more you are able and willing to acquire resources. If this is the case, then the rich countries are going to be richer as they get an increasingly bigger share of the pie, and the poor countries are going to be poorer as their share will be further grabbed by the rich.

Among all the resources in the world, human resources are the most valuable. Humans have used material resources and successfully converted them into objects that serve our daily living and further increase the ability to innovate and discover. Nature has given us the brains that have evolved into a miraculous learning machine driven by curiosity and pursuit of opportunity. Curiosity allows us to find the inner workings of atoms at the micro-level and the nature of the humongous structure of the universe at the macro-level.

The innovations in a short span of the last 100 years is no less than a miracle, but this pales in comparison to what is coming in the next 100 to 1,000 years. The world of the future is perhaps impossible to imagine accurately, as it was 100 years ago. Will this expansion of knowledge benefit all of mankind or just a subset of it? If the past is any predictor of the future, there is a case to be made that the benefit to human progress will be even more limited to a fraction of the world's population.

The basic human instincts evolved over thousands of years are hard-wired in the brain and are unchangeable. Humans want more, and to get that, they are willing to harm their opponents. The desire to acquire more does not stop at any stage, even after we have acquired significant wealth. Just look at the desire to accumulate wealth by the super-rich—they are still driven to get more even when nothing will change in their lives with the increasing wealth.

Humans are quite capable of vicious wars, indiscriminate killings, the subjugation of others, cruelty, insidious plots, and highly immoral acts for personal gain. Their ability and willingness to wipe out the enemy on a massive scale knows no limits. Just about 75 years ago, the world's biggest democracy did not hesitate to use atomic weapons to kill 200,000 people in two consecutive strikes. This tells us what could happen in the next 75 years as destructive capabilities has become available to those who are not bound to any democratic values with checks and balances.

Even more alarming will be the day when such destructive capabilities will be available to many groups, tribes, and nations. Some of them may have strong motivations to harm others—and this is not an if, but a when. The knowledge to acquire or steal nuclear, biological, or chemical weapons is widely available.

In the middle of all these possibilities is the availability of human capital. They will make things happen. Such human capabilities exist everywhere in the world, albeit proportionally less in the developing nations as compared to developed ones. Developed nations continue to acquire more human capital as more of the highly skilled professionals are willing to move to developed economies for significantly better opportunities.

This brain drain from the developing nations is another cause for creating inequalities in countries that require talented people the most. However, the developing and underdeveloped nations must create the right environment and the motivation to retain personnel and compete with the incentives of the brain drain. These countries must understand human needs and motivations.

The brain drain is motivated by financial well-being and better opportunities for people and their families. But moving to a completely new country is fraught with certain and uncertain risks. Leaving family and extended family, friends, and acquaintances to merge with a completely foreign environment and culture is awfully hard. I know this because I moved to the USA from Pakistan at the age of 26, leaving all my family and friends behind.

An equitable global agenda accounting for the elements discussed above is direly needed for the world to live in harmony and to avoid any flashpoint that will disintegrate the civilization.

## Business: Small, Medium, and Large

Everyone needs to work to produce income and make a living. Only a handful of people are independently wealthy and do not need to work, and I will talk about them later. It was not always like that. How did we get here?

Prehistoric hunter-gatherers never indulged in any so-called business for thousands of years, and yet they made a living. We hear stories of someone choosing to live an isolated life in a remote area while being resourceful enough to produce food to live independently. If only there was a way to get the things we need without buying them, then we wouldn't need to work, and there would be no business. If I need something that I cannot make or am not willing to make, someone has to make it for me and be compensated for their work. The concept of a business arises from this.

I can sit down and make a list of items I need. If I have them but did not produce them myself, then someone else must have made them. There are millions and millions of people who have needs like mine. So, millions and millions of the same items are made to fulfill the needs of all. For each item to be made, someone must set up a manufacturing plant. So, hundreds and thousands of manufacturing plants are set up by entrepreneurs.

In the beginning, before the invention of currencies, there was a barter system. If I have the skills to make an item, then I will make it and barter for another item that someone else made. This ensures everyone has everything through a barter system. But this was too cumbersome, so currency was invented.

Instead, I will give the item I made away for the units of currency someone is willing to pay based on the value of the item.

If there is a higher demand for the item I am making, then someone else will also make the same item to compete with me. They can make the item with higher or lower-quality materials and charge a higher or lower price. A person buying the item now has choices and will decide what to buy.

Businesses crop up based on marketplace demand. I make items, sell them, and buy items I need with the proceeds. The more items I sell, the more money I make, and the more items I can buy with my increased income. As an entrepreneur, I hire people to make all those items as I cannot do it all, and a business with employees is born. Everyone needs a bunch of items, so they will either create a business or work for a business to create those items.

With population growth, demands will be higher, along with the opportunities to establish businesses to fulfill the increased demand. With increased consumption and increased manufacturing, people will grow richer and demand more luxury or exotic items they do not really need but can now afford.

We are in a cycle of growth over the long haul. The middle class is growing. Some developing nations have made great advances in reducing poverty, while others are stagnant or declining. The tremendous upward spiral of wealth accumulation has shocked the world in many ways. Some are good, and others are not so good. The good part is that many are having good fortunes, but the bad part is that an overwhelming majority of the world's population is not so fortunate and facing decline and misery.

This is all about large businesses that have grown tremendously, destroying the small businesses in their wake. The businesses that have managed to become super large, and sometimes too large to fail, are monopolies for all practical purposes. As a result, they can steer the terms and policies for the operations of the business. They can command an even better competitive environment and associated growth, further pressing the small businesses to go belly up. Huge revenue and little to no taxes is the name of the game for large businesses. Their major shareholders have amassed unthinkable wealth.

As mentioned earlier, just eight individuals have a combined wealth that is more than the accumulated wealth of the poorer half of the population of the world. This lopsided distribution of wealth is accomplished under the umbrella of capitalism, while the rules of businesses are rigged by the few who wield tremendous power that stymies the opportunities for ordinary people. The already uneven playing field is systematically further rigged such that the entry barrier for small businesses is becoming higher.

Small businesses have historically provided most of the jobs and opportunities for higher income to at least the owners and key personnel. Medium-sized businesses are stuck between the large and small businesses, and are always on guard to justify their existence. Large businesses are ever ready to assimilate and devour the mid-size ones with impunity. Medium-size businesses that grow into large businesses is only a rarity. Typically, they are the feeder for the large businesses to become larger by mergers and accumulations.

We need to safeguard the vulnerability of small businesses against large businesses who can use the economy of scale to lower the price of products or services and thus assume tremendous market share. Large businesses can also artificially lower prices strategically for a short period, leveraging their large asset, and selling at a loss, even when the actual cost of the product or service is higher. This ploy, called dumping, may not be allowed, but loopholes are not too difficult to employ.

## The Problem with Someone Else Representing You

If you let someone represent you legally, then you need to give a legal authorization, in which case you spell out the scope of the representation. In the case of jointly selecting a person to represent you in the affairs of the State, it is a different matter. There is no legal binding that the person will truly work for the legislation that reflects your best interests. Of course, absent direct communication with the representative on the issue, there is no way for him or her to know your preference, except on a broader scale when campaigning. Thus, there is no guarantee you will be faithfully represented on each issue.

The fact is that no two people can have the same preference and opinion on every issue. There is no guarantee that pink will be a preferred color for any two individuals. Nor will be the choice of trousers, a shirt, or a tie. There is no certainty that two persons will equally support the increase of taxes, protection measures for the environment, equal rights for all ethnicities, free schooling for all, debt forgiveness of students, any restrictions on unlimited wealth distribution, care for the uninsured, role of religion in society, limited freedom for the security of state, and laws to support the poor and disadvantaged, to mention only a handful of an array of recurring issues we vote on.

The truth is people cannot be divided into black and white, as they come in all shades of color. Categorizing people into two, three, or four camps is as illogical as dividing people into zodiac signs based on when they were born. No two people have the same fingerprint, iris biometric recognition, face recognition, or DNA. Identical twins may have the same genes, but not the same gene expressions, and are thus vulnerable to different diseases. Even when growing up in the same family, they have different individual experiences and different beliefs.

How is it possible to encompass millions and millions of people into two, three, or even ten belief systems? Try only two predominant political belief systems in the USA and many other democracies in the world. Thus, millions of people are divided into two camps. If you ask one person, it is quite conceivable that his beliefs span over both parties on various issues. How can that person join one party or the other? I would venture to say that this will be the case with a significant part of the population.

The world cannot be divided into just a few camps when there are significantly divergent points of view. However, we pretend that such is the case—and build a world with such pretensions. What is stranger than people who are persuaded to wholeheartedly belong to one camp or the other? They dig in, go all or nothing, and forget who they are.

People, communities, states, and nations have committed—from time immemorial to this day—egregious acts of murder, torture, and human rights violations, justified by their perceived belief system. If the horror perpetuated is in the name of a belief system they are dug in and persuaded to follow it in totality, without any question and contrary to an individual's ethical values. In this case, the leadership of the representative must be questioned. Is the leader representing you in this instance? Obviously, he or she is not.

Democracy in its current incarnation is based on one individual representing you and thousands or millions of others. How is it possible to represent so many individuals while no two individuals are the same and may have different desires, outlook, and motivations in life? The only way this is possible is when all followers are sold on the same desires, outlook, and motivations in life, thus force-fitting thousands and millions into the same pigeonhole. That is the dilemma of inaccurate or false representation and remains essentially unquestioned.

The only other fully satisfactory approach is for each of us to represent ourselves. Can we directly vote on issues using a technology that is safe and hack-proof? Representative democracy has not worked for the overwhelming majority. We need to make an even playing field with changes to our institutions, disallowing so many middle persons making decisions for us with the use of our hard-earned tax money. The current systems are rife with loopholes that encourage unethical behavior and corruption, spearheaded by large corporations and wealthy individuals. Even when it might appear to be unthinkable now, I believe that solutions are possible with the use of the right technology in the future. Laws need to be changed and amendments made for the sake of transparency and fairness.

## The World Needs to Come Together

This idea may be centuries old, but it is perhaps more relevant today than at any time before. One thing is crystal clear: we are all on the same boat called the Earth. Contrary to popular belief, it is not only the superpowers who have something to say or offer but smaller countries as well. We are all connected quite intricately. Deforestation in the Amazon, pollution in Mumbai, nuclear power plant accidents in Chernobyl, Fukushima, and Three Mile Island, and a pandemic starting in Wuhan or Hong Kong each have global consequences. The global ecosystem connects every living thing through microbes.

The universe was created about 14 billion years ago by the Big Bang; the contents of the universe at the time of creation were hydrogen and helium. They congealed and formed galaxies. Then the stars were created, which had extremely high temperatures and pressures at their cores, where heavier elements were formed. All heavy material we see on earth and in the universe is the product of stars. Because of a supernova—the explosion of stars—these heavy materials are spread far and wide.

Earth's core does not have a furnace with temperature and pressure to bind lighter elements into heavier elements. Everything we see on this planet is the product of stars, including all elements of our body. The sun rays are the particles from the star, and plants grow because of the light coming from the universe. The food we eat is literally the product of the universe. Each time you eat, you can think of the food given to us from the heavens.

Sixty-six million years ago, a meteorite the size of a city hit the Earth, and made almost all the living things extinct, including dinosaurs who roamed in abundance. But this tragedy resulted in good news for us, as the small mammals blossomed and proliferated because the tyranny of the dinosaurs ended. The evolution of 66 million years resulted in modern-day humans, who now rule the Earth. Not only that, but humans are now bent upon destroying the Earth, given the prognosis by a significant number of scientists.

Mass extinctions are nothing new for the Earth. Five of them have been quoted frequently, and one was mentioned above. The worst occurred some 250 million years ago due to a prolonged and huge volcanic event releasing massive quantities of $CO_2$ into the atmosphere, resulting in the annihilation of almost all marine life and 70 percent of land life [10]. The recovery from this event took millions of years.

I have discussed pandemics before, but humans can carry plants and fungi from one place to another, such as using cargo containers, even when lots of restrictions are in place at this time.

Such movements have caused much havoc as the environment can be devastated by the introduction of new plants, fungi, animals, insects, and microbes.

One of the real threats is based on the fear that a hostile group, tribe, nation, or group of nations can invade an enemy population. This has already resulted in two world wars, killing millions of people and causing tremendous misery to many more. World War III has not occurred in the last 75 years, arguably due to the mutual threat of annihilation of the nuclear-armed countries, but there is no guarantee that it won't occur in the next 50 years. We have already witnessed several close calls, but no launch of nuclear warheads on the human population has taken place since the USA dropped two atomic bombs on Japan.

Globalization has brought countries and peoples together socially, economically, and politically. Unfortunately, social culture emanates only one way, from the developed to developing nation, and that has the effect of eroding the established and time-proven cultures in the East, without benefiting the Western cultures.

Economically, global trade by large multinational corporations has tightly integrated many business activities worldwide. Thus, a recession in the USA will filter through and impact the world. Any restrictions on the oil supply in the Middle East will readily impact the oil and consumer prices everywhere else. The stock market fluctuations propagating the world due to any direct or perceived events is an everyday phenomenon. Cross-country trade deals have quite a bit of impact on the economic well-being of every nation.

The world is quite connected politically. The World Trade Organization, United Nations, European Union, International Monetary Fund, and the World Bank, to name a few, have impacted political integration. The International Court of Justice, the judicial arm of the United Nations, deliberates global disputes and treaties between and among nations. However, the enforcement of international law is weak at best, and its effectiveness is based on the adherence of the nations to legal rules and to be part of the international community. However, it has been fragmenting recently. One severe flaw is that war is legal under international law to settle disputes and grievances, and allows the conquering of a nation by another nation. Extrajudicial decisions, without explicit agreement by the UN Security Council, to go to war, are not uncommon. Even punishment for severe war crimes resulting in the deaths of thousands of innocent civilians has been slow or unenforced. With all its flaws in the current structure, international bodies are somewhat of deterrence to blatant violations, and at least an embarrassment for powerful nations, or threat of retaliation for the weaker nations.

Socialism is no longer a significant dominant force, while democracy has been resilient and growing, where power stems from the people, not by kings, dictators, oligarchs, and plutocracy. In 1989, the Iron Curtain was torn down, and the Soviet Empire crumbled, along with the hegemony of communism. However, it still exists in China, Russia, Cuba, Vietnam, North Korea, and Laos; previously, the list included Afghanistan, Algeria, Belarus, Benin, Bulgaria, Cambodia, Congo, Czechoslovakia, Ethiopia, East Germany, Hungary, Mongolia, Mozambique, Poland, Romania, Somalia, Ukraine, North Vietnam, South Yemen, and Yugoslavia [11].

The promise of freedom and democracy has swept across the globe, and has overtaken communism and socialism, where power essentially rests with few. There are some 167 countries under varying democratic rule, out of 195 countries in the world. By 2018, more than 100 countries, mostly developing, have shown concrete economic progress [12].

Because the world is strongly connected, this is both an opportunity and a threat. The threat is quite significant as we continue to be weakened in various ways. This is the case if each nation, group, ethnicity, and tribe make decisions for their well-being in conflict with others, with a zero-some game in mind. That is the road to self-destruction in the long run. The connectedness also presents an opportunity to work together, rejecting the concept of winner takes all. We need to be able to compromise our take on excessive greed by corporations and individuals.

There is no reason for this greed, as beyond a certain point, hoarding of wealth by individuals or nations has no real benefit to the quality of life. The pursuit of excessive wealth or world domination is counterproductive, as following this path will ensure that, in the end, we will have nothing. We will wreck the environment, make this Earth inhabitable, lose everything we have built, along with all the philosophies and ideologies we continue to fight for in the pursuit of overtaking others.

## The Phenomenon of Critical Mass

People can spread an idea if it takes root in the consciousness of a certain percent of the population. It is suggested that it could happen if 10 percent of the population become diehard believers, dedicate themselves to the concept and stick with it. However, in the age of social media and electronic messaging, this percentage can be significantly lower, as a smaller group can muster tremendous reach with technology.

A unique or a new idea can take a long time to get some traction, or it can die. However, some ideas have universal appeal, which can catapult to be incredibly attractive if they reach a critical mass. This critical mass must consist of those who are convinced of the viability of the idea and willing to go the extra mile for the perceived benefit of the others.

The progression of acceptance can spread like wildfire after a tipping or turning point. Some of these ideas can be considered crazy or counter-intuitive when they first arise. To take these concepts and then persist and persevere is the key to reach the critical mass.

Let us say that I propose that a world government be created, with much more teeth than the United Nations, to govern peace in the world. The legislative power of this world government comes from the votes of the people in all the countries. Any critical decision is based on the referendum of the people. A hack-proof computerized database is created to account for the voters. Further, the referendum is done online, and it is foolproof.

Buy-in from the world's population provides the power to implement peace. The stakeholders are the inhabitants of the world. The decision of the world body is by referendum and supersedes the decision by any country.

The reason for such a world body is to make sure that:

- no country uses force to coerce or subjugate any other country.
- no country undermines its citizens and violates their human rights.
- no country makes or uses weapons of mass destruction.
- catastrophic events or acts of God such as earthquakes, wildfires, or tsunamis are addressed quickly and comprehensively.

Some of the processes, such as climate change, artificial intelligence, pandemic, and wealth inequality are addressed for the sustainability of humanity on Earth. Research and development are vigorously pursued for the well-being of all human beings.

Imagine the benefits of such a world government with the power of implementation and backed up by the population of the world. This will engender trust among the countries to the extent that unnecessary expenses on war machines and maintenance of the military will be significantly reduced. Substantial resources will free up, particularly among the world powers who have an inordinate budget for military buildup and maintenance. Even in the most powerful and rich countries of the world, about 5 to 18 percent of the population is relatively poor, the United States being at 17.8 percent [13]. In developing countries, more than 50 percent are poor [14]. Even the relatively poor countries have an inordinate budget for the military, as they do not trust their neighbors, and live under the constant fear that they will interfere and compromise their freedom, or harm them economically.

The world is in such a chaotic state that ideologies are ripping people apart. This has been in the making for decades. Our daily lives are severely contested by various groups, which threatens or further degrades living standards and quality of life. I have discussed it before, but the perceived fear of each other has made the world quite intolerable for much of the population.

Look around the world, and you will see the ever-increasing conflict zones, wars, and ideological clashes. Our intolerance of each other is quite remarkable. Invisible barriers, and sometimes real barriers, are becoming the norm, and the world is being sliced and diced in every which way.

I believe it is time for the citizens of the world to unite for the sake of a better and more peaceful world where factions among them are not confrontational, but synergistic for the well-being of all.

Now this idea may not be unique, as it resulted in the creation of the United Nations. However, the next step needs to be materialized with the help of citizens in the world.

If this concept is revolutionary, it is also quite attractive for the sake of sustainability of humanity on Earth. But this will require a critical mass of 10 percent or more of the world's population who will vehemently support the idea.

## The Root of the Problem

The problem starts from the very beginning—the early development of the child. The brain starts forming the kind of person he or she will become. Bit by bit, minute by minute, and hour by hour, a mental model of life take shape. Ethical values are absorbed from early interactions with family, friends, and the community. They start understanding right from wrong as early as two to five years old. A child is a great observer, even when he or she is unable to articulate. If the parents show strong ethics in their daily lives, that is what the child is going to accept. Of course, what they learn early will be reinforced or modified as they mingle with the community.

My contention is that the long-term and lasting solution for most of the world's issues is embedded in the right education for these young minds at the preschool to the primary school level. Strong ethics and a responsibility to humanity are developed at that stage, and that is lasting.

First, education is necessary to each child in this world—rich, middle-class, or poor. It must be steeped in dignity, respect, and justice for all human beings and the environment. The return on this investment is so high that it will pale in comparison to any other investment humanity can make.

After 20 to 30 years of investment in the education of children, there will be a generation who will have such empathy for humanity that trust among each other will be the currency that unites us. This is in contrast to a generation where competition and power-mongering over others is the currency, with little care for humanity and the environment. At this time, we have invented large corporations where the pursuit of profit runs supreme, overriding anything that comes in the way. Any attempt to fairly distribute wealth is resisted by policies and laws in collusion with the greedy in high offices. Businesses are inherently irresponsible socially and environmentally, and they have immunity by the misguided concept that democracy and capitalism encourage manipulation of laws to indulge in self-destructive behavior.

Countries have an inherent distrust of one another and indulge in military buildup at the expense of the well-being of their citizens. This is a curse that has resulted in immeasurable suffering and there is no stopping it. The money for militarism is robbed from the citizens who pay significant taxes for this continued misadventure. It would be a different world if we rebuild trust among the nations, take the incentives away from the reckless pursuit of confrontation in the name of ideology or domination over others, and agree to an equitable distribution of the world resources. Citizens will be much happier and less confrontational.

It all starts with individuals. The world will be a place that 7.8 billion people want. Well within every hundred years, the inhabitants are totally replaced. But the problem is that the seeds are contaminated by the mindset of fear, self-preservation, division, and tunnel vision. We need a generation of children who will be fearless, empathetic, inclusive, and open-minded. They need to care not for themselves, but also for others. They need to have a love for humanity.

We need children who grow up to innovate and use research and technology for the well-being of all. They would use the resources of the earth wisely. They would allow humane conditions for plants and animals. They would preserve the forests and freshwater resources. They would care about civility and human rights. They would think much less about creating weapons of mass destruction, and more about creating an environment for better health and happiness for all. They would think less about living in a home with triple locks, or sweeping the streets by mass incarceration, and more about treating each other humanely for better mental health for all. They would think less about making one-dollar hamburgers using the most inhuman way of mass production of cattle and chickens, and more about growing nutritious and safe food.

If you think that greed is the main ingredient that runs the economy, then you must also accept that greed is the engine that will serve as the demise of the Earth as well. This is because greed does not care about others, except when regulated to do so, and fair regulation is hard to come by as money, and the corruption that goes with the money will always tamper with just regulation.

The concept has nothing to do with socialism or communism, as they are the failed systems. If the pursuit of profit is capitalism, then the pursuit of satisfaction is the new capitalism for the next breed of world citizens. The pursuit of satisfaction would be more vibrant and acceptable, as the pursuit of pure greed has not delivered happiness to the masses.

The new breed of children should grow with the concept of attaining satisfaction and be enthusiastic about it. They should innovate and create for this purpose, instead of the vision of becoming super-rich. The old myth of college dropouts dominating the world by innovating a computer or other gadget should be debunked. The college dropout should now be a college graduate, still innovating, not for becoming super-wealthy, but for the satisfaction that such innovation brings substantial changes in the lives of the community or to humanity at large.

The world will change by allowing a new generation of children. These are the children who need to grow open-minded and enthusiastic about the goodness of humankind. They are voracious readers, critical thinkers, and creators of technology, vaccines, and healthcare systems that make sense. They will preserve the environment, instead of destroying it. For one thing, they will not be manipulators for personal benefits. They will understand that the world they live in is a privilege, and they should leave a slightly better world behind after their endeavors.

The new generation of children will understand the perils of insane profit. Yes, a person can live in a humongous home, and live a jet-set life, but at what expense, and with what incremental pleasure? The whole concept of the extreme rich does not make a whole lot of sense. In the end, you do not get much—unless life is spent to the benefit of mankind, as much as the pursuit of profit. That equates to remarkably high satisfaction. At the time of dying, no rich or powerful person can be so proud of the achievement attained by harming others or the environment.

There is truly little option for the survival of the Earth but to allow a new generation of children who will save us from our misdeeds, misadventures, and stupidity.

# The Tsunami That Will Devour Us

The grim reality is that fast-increasing growth is not good news, but bad news. With growth comes consumption of resources at a much higher rate than they can be renewed. The decision-makers who control Earth's resources are relatively few. Senseless mismanagement is happening now, but there are no signs that it will not further deteriorate soon.

Large multinationals have wielded their immense power to consolidate favorable policies to squeeze out the competition to acquire more wealth. Corporate greed knows no bounds, except the ever-burgeoning bottom line. The exploitation of human resources makes research and development possible to create unique products and services without equitably benefiting the personnel employed. The employees are the commodities who can be discarded whenever they become a burden on the company, no matter the past contributions. At-will employment is the policy *du jour* in most instances with no obligation to keep them in bad times.

It is all about what we want in society, and how we want to live. It seems like the need to acquire power and control over others is hard-wired in our brains (although it is not scientifically proven) and drives our motivation. Humans find it quite thrilling to be able to give orders to others, buy luxury cars, or large homes as less of a need but as proof they have arrived. The definition of success is rigged to mean how many things we can acquire, and how many human beings we can control.

This definition of success is so short-sighted and flawed that it has brought the world to a crossroads of terrible consequences. This has led us to ever-increasing growth to the extent that we are willing to degrade the environment and go broke to succeed. We are willing to succeed at all costs to find that we have nothing in the end.

Let us look at the need for ever-increasing energy to feed our growth. It is quite evident that large emissions of greenhouse gasses are contributing to the increase of Earth's temperature with severe consequences. But there is little appetite to backtrack or reverse that, as the future threat is not so palpable today. Meanwhile, we must supply electricity to keep building factories to feed the insatiable human consumption.

Will developed nations who contribute to the degradation of the environment the most actually cut back on their lifestyle of comfortable living? Or will they simply ask the other not so fortunate nations to slow down their progress and sacrifice to continue basic or even subsistence living? Will they impose on others not to eat meat, or cut down their forests, or not pollute the environment? When push comes to shove, it is quite likely that they will, given the history of how the powerful nations have plundered the unfortunate weaker nations and peoples, with impunity. "Might is right" has been the human motto since time immemorial, and it has not changed much to this date. I contend that the culprit is the definition of success as human beings. I can just say that definition of a nation is just an extension of the individual's definition of success—it is how much wealth the nation has and how much power it wields on other nations.

If the definition of success as individuals is flawed and leads to unintended consequences, then this definition of success as a nation is even more destructive. It will dramatically result in a human catastrophe—indeed, we are here in just about 200 years of incredible human progress. Imagine what could happen to us in many more centuries of following the same path?

The current definition of success will eventually lead to a tsunami that will devour us to extinction in the name of progress and achievement, and we will have nothing at the end.

## What Makes Life Miserable?

Let me define misery as the absence of happiness. We lead unhappy lives primarily based on ignorance and lack of education. Lack of education makes two things more likely: (1) invitations of exploitation, and (2) obstruction of the means to make decent wages and live healthy lives. It is quite clear that proper education is the key to avoiding miserable living; however, this is not a sufficient condition for happiness.

You can be educated and miserable. Further, by extension, I can also say that you can be educated and economically prosperous and can be miserable. On the contrary, if you are uneducated and poor, you are more likely to be miserable, although there are exceptions. However, it is quite established that poverty and happiness do not mix well.

Another major aspect is the psychological well-being that is generally formed quite early in life. Apart from genetic disposition, a major factor is being raised in a family where the child feels loved and secure. A broken family is a significant risk that negatively contributes to mental health issues in children and adolescents. The spouses in a broken family go through a miserable time, and the children may face trauma and be subjected to lifelong mental health problems.

Misery loves company, and one miserable person can cause a lot of pain to their immediate and extended family members, friends, and coworkers.

One may think a person born in a wealthy family has all reasons to be in a state of perpetual happiness. However, having no experience of a life other than a life of extreme comfort sucks the happiness away, if for no other reason than not understanding the displeasure of being poor. For that person, being wealthy is normal, without any overwhelming pleasure and joy in it. A poor person will have a true understanding and appreciation of wealth. So, before you become too envious of a wealthy person, consider the possibility that wealth itself is perhaps not that thrilling to a person in that position.

The life of the rich and famous may be fodder for viewing pleasure of a fantasy world, but the reality maybe something else. A child living in a slum may be as happy as the one in a very rich family because both know no better about the lifestyle of the other.

The excessive drive to become rich and famous perhaps takes a toll on real happiness, and it may not be worth the price. This is not the same as an accomplishment in scientific discovery, for example. Many Nobel Prize winners have no idea about winning until they are notified. In most cases, they have not been working all these years to be rich and famous. My contention is that we should not be eagerly devoting ourselves to the rat race of acquiring stuff for its own sake, of competing, or being in awe of others, just to be in a state of perpetual misery.

Many feel unhappy because they live their lives pretending to be someone they are not. That is called inauthentic living. We do not behave like ourselves and are always conscious of what others think. We may be presenting ourselves to please someone else and are not true to ourselves. Living inconsistently with our true selves can cause a great conflict within ourselves and make our lives perpetually miserable. The question to ask is, what is the worst that will happen if we present ourselves as we are? If the worst is acceptable, then we do not need to worry about it anymore, and happily live as we are.

## The Economic System that Preserves Us

Everyone needs food, clothing, and shelter. In addition, everyone has the right to realize their full potential. Economic systems have evolved to achieve this end. Among them all, capitalism has evolved to have a better track record of economic activities that aligns with a free and democratic society. Tightly run states that control citizens with an iron fist, on the other hand, are not as desirable.

However, capitalism has its own flaws—the inequitable distribution of resources and production is among the most serious ones. Capitalistic society has the danger of being controlled by the wealthy elites who are most influential in creating policies most favorable to them. Money dictates politics, and the poor have little say, even when they are supposedly free to elect the representative who will protect their rights to make a decent living.

Elected representatives are mostly wealthy people, educated at elite schools, articulate, and very savvy in exploiting the less educated ordinary people. In many cases, deceptive approaches are the tools of the elites to gain power over the masses. They collude with the like-minded influential people to jointly climb up the ladder or to stay at the upper echelon.

The principal reason that some people will do anything to retain or gain more wealth or power is insecurity or a mindset of deficient life. The human brain has been hard-wired to be insecure about their next meal and to fear constant threats to their lives. I believe that this built-in insecurity is the prime motivator to create an artificial mindset of perpetual deficiency, no matter how much we have. We are engaged in a dog fight to grab resources, by any means, mostly under cover of legal authorization, and in some cases, even by violating the established rules we have made.

In a capitalistic society, the more we have, the more we want to have. Profit is the prime motivator, which fuels the economic system in defiance of those who cannot make it. The theme is not to care for all, but for the few who succeed. Assets are not taxed, but income is. Thus, people who have become rich and have large assets pay little taxes in proportion to poor people who do not have assets but live by income through wages, which are taxed. In this economic system, the rich become richer by virtue of their assets, and the poor become poorer because they have insignificant assets.

The few who make it to the top in leadership positions have no idea how the poor live, except at a superficial level. For example, there are those who have never visited a grocery store or have no idea how much meat costs per pound, yet they have been relegated to take care of most of the population.

In a society where profit is the prime motivator, the environment is less of a concern because environmental protection is costly. Corporations would rather spend money to produce bigger returns to the shareholders, so they become richer more quickly.

There have been corrections in a handful of economies in Europe—which have a very small population-- made to this highly inequitable democratic system, by introducing the limits and incentives to those who achieve power. Wealth is distributed somewhat equitably by higher taxes to the wealthy and corporations. Assets are taxed so the rich do not become super-rich by default, and the poor do not become poorer. Human dignity and rights are preserved by providing health care and education to all. The greed of individuals and corporations are contained. Each person gets a safety net of living expenses in case they lose their income. However, most existing economies are quite punitive to the well-being of most of the world's population.

We must adhere to an economic system that sustains all the people globally and not just for a few. Inequality will stir discontent and rebellion, eventually devouring all we have. Then we will be left with nothing to fight for.

## Genetically Engineered Humans

Genetic engineering manipulates DNA for the benefit of mankind, but its implications on the future of the world are like something out of a science fiction novel. We have already increased the yield of some of the crops significantly, and in the future food shortages may be eliminated entirely.

Gene therapy has a real promise to cure many debilitating illnesses, providing a major boost to the quality and longevity of human life.

Genetic splicing can produce the proverbial designer babies, ushering in a golden age of superhumans. Evolution by nature will be obsolete, and humans will eventually be in full control of this process.

Too much of every good thing has the potential of abuse, and genetic engineering is no exception. Are we going to embark on producing superhumans who will rule the world of lesser humans? Will the world embark on a race, like we have seen of nuclear proliferation, to dominate with superhumans? Who will start this race, and who will develop the most superior and efficient technology to produce the best superhumans?

These superhumans will not be robots, but real humans, like you and I, but with much superior intellect, physical looks, and fitness. The capabilities of the "natural" humans will dwarf in comparison to humans designed to have superior traits through genetic engineering.

Should we restrict progress in genetic engineering so we do not develop the technology to produce a superior race that will eventually take over the world?

We know that we cannot do that. We are not capable of restricting or reversing human progress in science and technology. Moving forward is inevitable. Momentum will only build as we move down the slippery slope.

Again, this is the *déjà vu* of nuclear energy at the beginning, where the technology produced controlled nuclear reactions that are useful for electrical power plants—after America detonated atomic weapons at Hiroshima and Nagasaki. Soon, the technology resulted in building more deadly nuclear weapons among rich nations, and some poor nations. Now, we have these weapons of mass destruction that can annihilate the world many times over. It is quite reasonable to assume that once you have the capability, you will eventually use it. It is simply the question of when, not if. The same will be the case of genetically re-engineered humans.

Once the technology is there, it is only a matter of time when such humans will arrive through genetic interference and take over the world. In the meantime, we can continue to use technology to benefit agriculture and healthcare.

## Threat from Artificial Intelligence

The incredibly fast pace in the advancement of computer coding has given rise to artificial intelligence, the code that can itself create code independent of human interference and learn from human and environmental input. Apple's Siri, Amazon's Alexa, various automatic language translators, and speech recognition apps all use AI.

We have been obsessed with the concept of machines taking over humans and imposing their interests in conflict with us. Literature and movies are replete with stories of machines close to taking control of resources in our world for their goals of world domination.

However, many scientists do not rule out such possibilities. Machines will develop the capabilities to keep learning and become better at self-programming and decision-making. Machines can learn and make decisions much faster than organic brains, thus making it quite plausible to collectively surpass human intelligence. It is said that all humans need to do is to pull the power plug, making the machines useless. But a highly intelligent machine can run all the possible scenarios quite easily that would incapacitate them and make amends to avoid this fate.

We are already quite dependent on apps that use machine learning, even when we are in complete control of the machines. The rise in AI technology is fast and furious, and the time of its role to advance and supersede human intelligence is not farfetched. We already show quite a bit of dependence on AI with voice and face recognition activities. We rely on decision-making based on input parameters on algorithms that keep improving with time. With time, AI will lead our daily lives and almost all aspects of work, blurring what we decide and what a machine decides for us.

As we get up, the whole daily agenda will be ready for us. Our diet, exercise, work tasks, social life, retirement portfolio, and leisure plans will be done without much of our interference. Soon, we will be machines guided by AI. We will, out of laziness or necessity, relinquish substantial parts of our lives to the invisible gods, omnipresent to help us get through. All of the interconnected aspects of our lives will become so difficult. They will require several dimensions of our thinking, best relegated to the software that will crunch the numbers to get the optimum solution. There will be no way to get better decision-making tools in a more complicated information-driven world than the self-generating, self-correcting, and exponentially improving AI.

If AI will rule, the future world remains to be seen. We know that AI's role is ever-increasing, and we cannot rule out a world relegated to this sobering possibility.

## Nuclear Proliferation

Because I have a master's degree and Ph.D. in nuclear engineering, that I obtained many decades ago, I was frequently asked if I would be working in the nuclear weapons industry. The answer was truly clear in my mind from the get-go: I will pursue a career in the peaceful uses of nuclear technology. As a nuclear engineer, I started my career in the area of risk assessment related to accidents in nuclear power plants, working in the area of mathematical models rather than in the operations. However, the dangers were always on my mind, and I wrote a paper on the risk of nuclear proliferation compared to other societal risks.

With the advent of nuclear detonations in Nagasaki and Hiroshima, we are on a constant alert of its wartime use. Far more dangerous and powerful nuclear bombs have been created since then, and in large numbers by several countries. Deterrence of mutual annihilation is cited as the reason why any other nuclear bomb was not used to kill civilians.

If you think the workings of nuclear weapons are a secret, you may be surprised to hear it is not. The theoretical basis of building atomic weapons is well known. However, the technology of uranium enrichment and detonation is not that easy. This means that it would be hard for a rogue terrorist organization to make a nuclear bomb that can be detonated. However, making a "dirty bomb" laden with radioactive material is quite possible. They only need to steal adequate quantities of radioactive material, say from a radioactive disposal site, and detonate that by conventional means in the middle of a dense population to create havoc.

It is only a matter of time until many more countries have nuclear weapons if there is no dramatic reduction in the lack of trust and animosity among the nations. There is little evidence that the international divide separating haves and have-nots, rich and poor, mighty and weak, and high tech and low tech is going to bridge the gaps. Rich nations are not showing any readiness to bring along the poor ones and are ready to exploit resources wherever they are available through diplomacy, arm-twisting, or blatant use of military might. None of these are conducive to discouraging or abandoning the zeal of non-nuclear countries to seek nuclear weapons as deterrent to exploitation.

Nuclear proliferation is a particularly big threat from nations that have accumulated huge amounts of ready-to-go nuclear bombs and materials, enough to destroy the Earth many times over. Human error, miscalculation, and faulty systems can launch a barrage of all-out nuclear war. Further, a rogue or mentally derailed head of state of these nations could cause a catastrophe. We only have data for the last 75 years, which may not be the predictor for human wisdom and restraint for the next 75 years. We might have to pay the ultimate price as many more nations go nuclear for one reason or another.

## Climate Change

On November 14, 2019, the visual of the City of Venice underwater was quite dramatic. The same could be the scene in the lowlands of Bangladesh. In fact, half the world could eventually be in danger. The rising temperature of the Earth is melting the ice caps, resulting in rising sea levels.

Despite the consistent and relentless warning of scores and scores of scientists, humans are in denial and unwilling to tackle the issue head-on. There is no willingness to roll back on the emission of greenhouse gasses.

Unfortunately, after a rise of just a few degrees of Earth's temperature, the roller coaster impact on sea-level rise, frequency and severity of hurricane generation, forest fires, extinction of species, and the quality of the lifestyles that we will be relegated to, will have little recourse.

To reduce greenhouse gases, we need to go back and take a hit on several fronts. Some of the significant ones are as follows:

- The release of $CO_2$ emissions from the coal-fired power plants must be curbed.
- The release from the animal farms must be reduced as we switch our diets to eat more vegetables and less meat.
- Deforestation must be stopped, and a huge number of trees must be planted.

- The refrigerant dispersion in the air must be totally curtailed.
- The number of cars must be reduced.

All this is expensive, particularly in the face of the growing population. Each new person added to the planet would need resources for survival and for the quality of the life each of us strives for: everyday things (such as housing, furniture, electricity, clothes, and food) and luxury items (such as electronic devices, jewelry, car, and air conditioning). We would need to either eliminate or curtail the use of many of these items in the current form and perhaps find alternatives that are not as taxing to the environment.

All indications are that not much time is left for significant corrections, and we are heading to the eventual—and likely unavoidable—collision course. That is unless extremely aggressive course correction is undertaken in a hurry to reduce the impact.

## Environmental Degradation

Polluting the air, water, and soil has devastating effects on the health and safety of human beings and all other species coexisting on Earth. We have managed to significantly compromise the air quality by continuously emitting vast quantities of harmful gasses and particulates. We pollute rivers and the sea by dumping toxic waste. We erode soil by cutting trees.

Earth's diameter is 8,000 miles, but the atmosphere is only about 62 miles high (this is the Karam line, beyond which atmosphere mingles with space). This is comparably quite thin and cannot be guaranteed to withstand the onslaught of relentless human activities. With an odd mix of 78 percent nitrogen and 21 percent oxygen (plus the remaining 1 percent consisting of $CO_2$, water vapor, and other substances), our atmosphere is quite unique compared to any other heavenly bodies.

Planets like Earth in other solar systems lose atmosphere early on as they revolve around highly active stars. The young active stars emit electromagnetic fields resulting in x-rays and ultraviolet radiations that knock-off the atmosphere. Only one planet we know of, Earth, has plants that produce food via photosynthesis and produce oxygen. Trace amounts of oxygen are present in the planets Mercury and Mars, but have no plant life.

We do not want to deplete the ozone layer present in the upper atmosphere because of chlorine and bromine gases being released either from industrial or personal use. Although the current lockdown due to the novel coronavirus has the effect of patching the ozone layer holes at an unprecedented level, this is certainly temporary, until the world's economy starts in full force again.

## For Whom the World Glitters

Just go to the Dubai Mall in the United Arab Emirates and walk around. One day is perhaps not enough to browse some 1,300 retail stores, offering an incredible array of exquisite and expensive products. Who can afford products from Dubai Mall or any other similar places? Now, about six billion people earn

$10 per day or less [8] [15]. Only about 10 percent of the world's population is high income, making $50 per day or more [16].

In a rich country like the USA, 25 percent of Americans make $100 per day or less [17]. Obviously, all the glitter is for the top 10 percent of the world's population at best.

If 10 percent are the beneficiaries, then there is a deeper problem. Are the world's natural resources up for grabs for the top few percent, while they are denied to the rest? The argument could be that the beneficiaries are the ones who created the glitter by their ingenuity, hard work, and risk-taking—they are the deserving ones. Thus, as the rich justify, the world glitters for the few who created it. We need to pause and think deeply about this justification, as everyone else is not so thrilled about it.

## When Men Think They are Created Superior

Nature has given men two advantages over women. They are physically stronger, and they do not give birth. Women must nurture the newborn for months and years, and thus are less available to participate in outside labor. Men have taken advantage of and relegated women to the subservient position from time immemorial until now.

In advanced societies, some of these inequities have been cured as women have secured more human rights, such as voting, but much remains unequal. Some of them are given unequal pay for the same job, are subject to the glass ceiling in corporations with scant high-level positions, face sexual harassment in workplaces, limited reproductive rights, and experience high incidence rates of rape at college campuses and beyond.

In developing nations, where reforms on gender equality are dubious, women still work more combined hours at work and at home but are economically poorer. This causes the country to be poorer as well.

It is men who are mostly responsible for the sex trafficking of women and children by creating a vigorous market for it. In wealthier countries, the traffickers make huge profits as the wealthier men are willing to pay substantial money for this service. In Western countries, the victim can generate annual revenue for their masters of $80,000 and in the Middle East $55,000, by some account. In the USA, illegal massage parlors may have sex-trafficked victims and can have an average of 12 visitors per woman per day, charging $60 per visit by one account. Of course, the customers are all men [18].

One in three women anywhere will have an incidence of sexual violence in their lifetime. Guess who perpetrates this violence?

Female genital mutilation is a major human rights violation, and an estimated 200 million girls and women are currently living with this affliction [19]. There are various reasons, including social and religious, but the rules are made and perpetuated by men in the affected countries. Women have been systematically killed by their own family members by the hundreds every year in various countries, in many cases with impunity. About 12 million early child marriages take place every year [20].

It is hard to explain this behavior, but perhaps men are hardwired to the acts of misbehavior and violence towards women over millions of years of evolution. Men's impulsive and sometimes reckless behavior to engage in short-term, casual sex has created a world hostile to women and the fabric of civilized society. In many instances, men are just not able to make rational decisions when a predatory instinct kicks in with a willing or unwilling partner. This may explain why men continue to violate the human rights of women to this date. Whatever the justification, men cannot be absolved of this systematic, barbaric, and brutal behavior. Like Jimmy Carter, the former U.S. President concluded, "In general, men don't give a damn." [21]

## The Bottom Two Billion People

This is the incredible story of the bottom 25 percent of the world's population, 7.8 billion in 2020, or about 2 billion people. About 663 million children (about 1 in 3) live in households that are poor, lacking necessities such as nutrition or clean water. Out of them, 356 million children (1 in 5) live in extreme poverty. About 1 billion children are multidimensionally poor, meaning that they lack necessities such as nutrition or clean water. Further, 150 million additional children plunged into poverty due to COVID-19 [22]. Subsistence living with scant resources and little ownership of anything is their fate—the same that they had for generations.

They have little idea about nutrition and healthcare. They are unaware of their true standing and rights and not knowledgeable about the steps needed for any upward mobility. They are hardly literate, with little formal schooling. They make their living basically from unskilled manual labor. Most of them live in South Asia and sub-Saharan Africa.

In many countries, even when extreme poverty has reduced dramatically, the widening wealth gap has relegated the poor to the income level of $1.50 to $2.50 USD per day.

I find it quite perplexing that the one thing that could impact the poverty reduction had not taken place at utmost priority in the last 50 years. Many of these poor nations do not educate their children through primary schools. This lack of priority to education has relegated many nations as the lower class, unable to create the educated population to make a dent into economic uplifting.

I believe that there is a rather quick fix, in the time scale of no more than three to four decades, to take a country from low education to higher education among a significant population. It needs to be articulated and agreed upon that no matter what the current status of a nation, compulsory high-quality primary and secondary education should not only be a policy on paper, but implemented with a zeal like nothing else.

The true return on investment will come with higher education. A large population would acquire the necessary skills with higher education to take the country to much sought after economic progress.

A huge investment in education to make a significant difference in four decades—that will last forever? I would take it. I discuss more on this topic later.

## Plastic Will Inherit the Earth

Plastic is everywhere. The most convenient and low-cost packaging material, created in 1907, was made popular in the 1960s. Before that, clay or glass was used as a molding material. Supermarkets in the USA started switching from paper to plastic bags in 1982. In a short period of 30 to 40 years, plastics have polluted the land, rivers, and oceans to an extent unimagined before. The plastic used is not biodegradable and its toxic impact will last for hundreds and thousands of years.

Disposable, single-use plastic bags have been banned or restricted in about 90 countries, including Bangladesh, China, Italy, Rwanda, the Congo, Kenya, and South Africa [23]. Several states such as North Carolina and Hawaii, as well as states in India and Australia, have also done the same.

Despite all the hoopla about recycling, right now only about 20 percent of plastics are recycled yearly; the rest are discarded, or incinerated, causing havoc for the environment with severe health effects. So far, only about 9 percent of plastics produced since 1950 have been recycled [24]. The main disposal methods are landfills—that is a source of continuing hazard—and some incineration, which emits toxic chemicals very hazardous to human health.

The extensive use of plastics has resulted in toxic chemicals in the blood and tissues of almost all living human beings. Some 95 percent of humans have detectable levels of bisphenol A (BPA) in their urine that can affect fertility, reproduction, and other processes in the human body. Toxic chemicals are leached into the soil, reaching the groundwater that ultimately goes into the water that we and all other species consume. Microplastics can spread through microorganisms to all places of the world with unknown but potentially devastating consequences.

More than 80 percent of the tap water sampled around the world contains microplastics. Tap water in the USA is found to be among the most polluted of the advanced nations [25].

Huge quantities of plastic debris, about 8 million tons every year, and some 100 million tons so far, have polluted the oceans, killing an unprecedented number of marine animals. They include fish, turtles, and seabirds. In the Pacific Ocean, the ocean currents have created three islands of debris, called the Great Garbage Patches, which are visibly quite disturbing.

The main source of plastics in landfills are single-use plastic bags, packaging, water bottles, and other items.

In 50 years, it is projected that there will be more plastic in the ocean than fish [26]. There are 300 million tons of plastic produced every year, half of them are for disposable single use [27]. About one million plastic bottles are bought every minute in the world, and 91 percent is not recycled [28]. In the USA alone, Americans throw away 35 million plastic water bottles every year [29].

We must stop the plastic madness at the very source by significantly reducing production. Other approaches to plastic wrappers and bags must be used. Large petrochemical companies are not going to do that, as the current incentives and laws do not warrant them. They are also unlikely to take a hit on their high-profit margin. We have discussed this before, as large businesses have a lot of power, including legally allowed lobbying and political activism.

## The Gene Drive

Genetic engineering is destined to change the genetic composition of some of the species of Earth forever, and perhaps irreversibly. Some of these changes are going to help mankind significantly, as the cure for malaria by changing the genes of mosquitoes so malaria cannot be spread. On the other hand, the long-term impact of many of these changes will not be known, and some of them would have destructive implications. World bodies are unanimous about being cautious. Regulations are being put in place so the genetically modified species will not be released without approval or safeguards. However, like many other destructive instincts and implementations, the regulations and cautionary tales will always not be followed by all.

It is almost certain that there will be scientists, groups, and nations who will break the rules, and make some of the species either extinct, or change them for good. There is no doubt that someone will experiment with humans, even when the whole human race cannot be mutated or modified through gene drive. Designer babies are another story that I have discussed before.

There is little doubt that many will try to create babies with chosen characteristics.

Will there be malicious use of gene drive? The brutal historical instincts of humans show that we have left no stone unturned in order to harm others for the sake of self-preservation or self-interest. The use of gene drive to harm others would be no exception.

The technology to manipulate genes on a mass scale is here, like atomic, chemical, and biological weapons. Even when the technology for gene drive is invented for the well-being of humankind, it has unleashed one of the greatest threats possible.

This is another example of how humans have used their ingenuity to create technologies that will eventually be turned against them. We have this gift of creativity, yet we have a dark side that borders on stupidity. We cannot let go of the dizzying speed of perceived progress, ahead of human flaws and errors. How many fatal technologies are we able to dodge, and for how long?

## The Irony of Growth

Growth is a recurring obsession and the measure of the success of the economy. The stock market certainly gyrates on the basis that any slowdown is bad news. But growth may not convey the rosy picture we take for granted.

Ironically, there is a wide disconnect in consumption between developed and developing nations. For example, compared to the USA, average household expenditures in India is 11 percent, Bangladesh is 7 percent, and China is 15 percent [30].

As discussed before, population growth is the highest in developing nations, where some 1.3 billion people live in 104 countries, which account for poverty at various levels [31].

All population growth is not created equal; there is a wide disparity as to which growing population will destabilize the world. In fact, population growth in developing nations can increase several-fold, and it would still not make a dent in the sustainability of the world's resources. It is the population and population growth in developed nations that is the threat to world sustainability.

The topics related to growth that follow are applicable only to the high-consumer countries.

### Electricity

Electricity is the building block for the growth of a country, as without an adequate supply of it, there cannot be new factories, homes, or office buildings. We would need more electrical power plants to produce electricity, that may require the burning of fossil fuel (which is the most prevalent to create electricity all over the world), which pollutes the environment with greenhouse gasses and other byproducts, including particulates. People inhale this stuff and become sick. So, in addition to global warming, we have a health crisis.

There are cities where pollution has become unbearable at times. There are thousands of adults and children who suffer from pollution-related illnesses. Yet, there will be no growth without high consumption of electrical energy. The alternatives to fossil fuel power plants have not become viable yet as a significant replacement. Thus:

More growth >> more electricity consumption >> more pollution >> more global warming and sickness >> decline in sustainability on Earth.

### Meat Consumption

Meat production comes at a high cost. First, it requires remarkably high consumption of water—about 2,500 gallons of water to produce one pound of beef (in comparison, soybeans consume 216 gallons and corn 108 gallons of water). In addition, one pound of beef requires the equivalent of one gallon of gasoline and 35 pounds of grain (mostly soybeans, corn, and other grains) [32].

The strain on freshwater resources, and energy, by the sheer level of high meat production, is tremendous because feeding an ever-growing world population may not be sustainable in the long run.

How can we contain meat production in the face of the growing demand? Many have touted the health effects of the large consumption of meat in our diet. In contrast, others espouse eating more plant-based diets. Yet, I am not sure that it is possible to change this behavior in the foreseeable future to lower the impact of the dietary habit of high rates of meat consumption.

More growth >> more meat consumption >> more drain on freshwater resources and energy>> decline in sustainability on Earth.

**Cutting the Branch You are Sitting On**

About 44 mature trees need to be cut to build the average 2,600-square-foot American home. It takes 60 years to grow an 80-foot fir tree, and 44 trees cut for a home will require 2,640 tree-years to replenish the loss.

It is estimated that the world needs to build two billion homes in the next 80 years, which will require 88 billion trees; even if the house sizes are halved, the requirement would be 44 billion trees [33].

While it is estimated that there are 3 trillion trees in the world, they are shrinking due to deforestation at a net loss of 10 billion trees per year. An estimated 1 trillion trees will be lost in 80 years, one-third of the existing tree population.

It takes seven or eight trees to produce enough oxygen to sustain one person. That means we need, for the world's population of 10 billion in 2100, about 70 billion trees. Fortunately, trees are not the only means of producing oxygen; 70 percent of the world's oxygen is produced by algae and other marine animals through photosynthesis.

Plants absorb carbon dioxide. A mature tree absorbs about 48 pounds of $CO_2$ per year. Global $CO_2$ released to the environment is about 37 billion tons per year [34]. Of the $CO_2$ released, 25 percent is absorbed by trees and plants, 25 percent is absorbed by the ocean, and 50 percent remains in the atmosphere [35]. We require half a trillion mature trees to absorb 25 percent of atmospheric $CO_2$. If we want to take out another 25 percent from the atmosphere, then another half a trillion mature trees will be required. So, the existence of one trillion trees is a good idea for $CO_2$ absorption and $O_2$ emission for sustainability. However, the balance can be easily broken if deforestation or emissions increase. By all accounts, the net $CO_2$ is rising at a faster rate.

$CO_2$ has never exceeded 300 parts per million (ppm) in the past million years; by mid-1700s, it was 280 ppm; by 1958, it was 315 ppm; in 2013, it was 400 ppm; in 2015, it exceeded 400 ppm. By the end of this century, it is projected to increase to 900 ppm [36].

Which brings us to the emphasis of planting trees as a good idea, but it takes decades before a tree matures, plus if we solely rely on tree planting, then we will run out of land to keep the $CO_2$ at the sustainable level. It is quite certain that deforestation and man-made emissions will further increase this greenhouse gas in the atmosphere soon. Further, it will change the rainfall pattern. There will be less rain in some areas, and flooding due to heavy rainfall in other areas. Wildfires in forests are possible in other areas. In fact, unprecedented fires are burning in California as I am writing this passage.

One of the great casualties of deforestation is the dramatic decline of the animal population by 60 percent in the last 40 years, according to the World Wildlife Federation's Living Planet Report from 2018—they include mammals, birds, fish, reptiles, and amphibians.

"This report sounds a warning shot across our bow," said Carter Roberts, president and CEO of WWF-US. "Natural systems essential to our survival—forests, oceans, and rivers—remain in decline. Wildlife around the world continues to dwindle. It reminds us we need to change course. It's time to balance our consumption with the needs of nature, and to protect the only planet that is our home."

The high frequency of forest wildfires and devastation the world over, including recent ones in California, Brazil, Australia, and Indonesia, are mostly the result of hotter and drier weather caused by climate change. The unusual heat in the Arctic, such as Alaska and Siberia, is especially troubling as unusual amount of long-preserved carbon is threatened to be released:

Forests wildfires >> $CO_2$ emission >> climate change >> hotter and drier weather >> more forests wildfires.

In addition, many drugs have been successfully produced from the trees in forests, and there is quite a bit of promise for future drug discovery—and that promise will be jeopardized:

More growth >> more coal fired power plants, houses, cars, roads >> more deforestation >> more $CO_2$ >> more global warming.

## T-Shirts, Jeans, Eggs, Milk [37]

It takes about 713 gallons of water to make a t-shirt [38]. Washing one load in a washing machine requires 40 gallons of water—drying them requires five times more energy.

Just the cotton grown for a pair of jeans takes about 1,800 gallons of water. After dying and machine washing, it takes a total of 9,982 gallons of water.

It requires 53 gallons of water to produce an egg—as chicken feed is water-intensive.

To produce one gallon of cow milk, it takes 2,000 gallons of water.

To produce one pair of shoes requires 2,257 gallons of water.

More growth >> more t-shirts, jeans, eggs, milk >> more freshwater consumed >> less availability >> shortage of freshwater.

Developed nations should be very conscious of unnecessary consumption that pits consumerism against environmental constraints. Affordability is not the only issue; it is the depletion of the resources for their children, grandchildren, and great-grandchildren. Plus, it is punishing the poor in the developing nations for no fault of their own; they did not even enjoy the consumption and are being harmed by the environmental degradation and lack of freshwater resources for nothing.

## Bottled Water for Sale

Big businesses are taking water from the tap and repackaging it for sale. And we are only happy to buy it in hordes. All they do is to distill the water and put them in good-looking plastic bottles with attractive colorful labels, depicting mountains with snow caps and waterfalls. Most of the bottled water is not from any spring, contrary to the claim. Some are pumped from underground, but they can label that as spring water, as long as they are connected underground to any spring.

We are buying bottled water for one predominant reason: Tap water is alleged contaminated and perhaps bad for our health. Nothing is further from the truth. In fact, the contents of tap water are regulated and tested daily as they are released for drinking, yet there is no regulation for testing the so-called spring water sold in bottles.

The most bothersome part is not the water in the bottle, but the bottle itself. First, the chemicals leaching from the plastic bottles may be harmful. It goes into our bloodstream and may cause such health problems as diabetes, obesity, high blood pressure, and cancer. Second, plastic is an environmental nightmare, as I have discussed before. In the United States alone, more than 60 million plastic bottles are discarded every day. Some 22 billion of them clog the waterways and pollute the ocean in one year. Worldwide, a million plastic bottles are sold every minute. The energy required to produce one bottle of water is 2,000 times of the same amount of tap water.

More alarming is that the water bottles are being touted as the solution for the water shortage in the developing nations where drinking water is in short supply, such as Yemen, Libya, Jordan, Western Sahara, Djibouti, Nigeria, and Pakistan. The underground water is pumped and purified to fill the bottles, depleting much of the water resources underground.

It all stems from the lack of fresh water; more than one billion people lack access to fresh water. One reason is the scarcity of fresh water to begin with. Seventy percent of the world is covered with water, but only 2.5 percent of it is fresh water; the rest is undrinkable as it is saline and ocean-based. About two-thirds of the freshwater is locked in the ice caps, and when they melt, they flow mostly unused to the ocean. Thus, there may be enough fresh water for the world's population, but it is not accessible to all people, and a significant portion that is available is polluted. Lack of management of water resources, population growth, and man-made waste are the primary reasons. In any case, the lack of natural freshwater has provided an opportunity to the water-bottling mega businesses to extract underground water, purify it, fill plastic bottles and sell to those who do not have access to fresh water. Many are impoverished population who can ill afford it.

It is imminent that states find a solution to clean up the freshwater resources from contamination, stop any waste dumping, and make drinking water accessible to all. If big businesses can exploit and fill the gap for their profit, I do not see why the states and countries are unable to do that. Laws and regulations should be for the public benefit and not for public exploitation to make the rich even richer for no real purpose (remember, as any incremental wealth to them does not increase their happiness and fulfillment in any case).

In the process, we must stop creating more single-use water bottles clogging the waterways, land, and oceans, as this is creating a dangerous safety problem for all living beings on Earth.

## Can We Afford to Keep Growing?

It is now quite established by many responsible boards of directors, shareholders, and owners of businesses that sustainable growth is the criteria upon which all strategic and operational decisions must be made. But an overwhelming number of businesses are going forward with the status quo—grow as much as possible, in the shortest period.

The world economy is based on the pursuit of growth. For one thing, the stock market rewards those who consistently grow and penalizes those who do not. With a tightly integrated world economy, a slowdown in China or Japan will impact business in the USA, for example. And surely, any slowdown in the USA will have a negative effect across the world. However, as I have discussed the dire consequences of unchecked growth earlier, the dilemma appears to place us between a rock and a hard place.

If we accept that unlimited growth in developed economies is not an option, then we need to decide what sacrifices we can make, so we leave an ecologically sound Earth to our children and grandchildren.

We are used to or compelled to use several cars in a family, most of the time because the public transportation may be bad or non-existent, and we need transportation to work. We buy clothes even when we can easily do without an additional t-shirt, a pair of jeans, or a pair of shoes. We buy equipment or gadgets sometimes unused or redundant. We buy the biggest home we can afford, or even when we cannot really afford it. The fact is that, on average, Americans have about 300,000 items and they use only a fraction of them on a consistent basis, and even outspend other developed nations by far on toys for children [39].

However, the problem is that if a substantial population stops buying frivolous, unneeded, and redundant things, then the economy will slow down. Factories will be closed, home and car buying will slow down, the insurance industry will suffer, doctors' offices will have fewer patients, businesses will go bankrupt, employees will be laid off, and much more. That is not a pretty picture.

Is slowdown or reversal in growth a catastrophe that will devour human progress and substantially reduce the living standards the world over? Perhaps, but not the world over. Eighty percent of the world's population already has quite marginal living standards, compared to the rest of the 20 percent. So, if the standard of living of the top 20 percent suffers, it will be devastating. But the further slippage in the earning of the rest of the 80 percent will be catastrophic, as that will drive up the poverty level, perhaps on par with the subsistence level.

As continuous growth at the present rate is non-sustainable, we have little choice but to tamp it down for the sake of survival. But that prognosis is difficult to digest for the rich. There is little chance that the rich will give up growth. The top 10 percent is used to relentless growth. They would rather close the borders and live in the gated community, caring less about the rest of the world.

The other thought is that the rich will soon realize that hoarding all the riches and letting the poor bear the brunt of environmental degradation and resource depletion will be catastrophic to themselves. They would be unlikely to survive in isolation. The best case for survival is to bring all the world inhabitants along, as we are all in the same boat, and if the boat sinks, we all drown.

Thus, we all need to slow down and tread the middle ground. Grow cautiously. Just stop being extravagant. Instead of buying two shirts, buy one. And that goes for pants, shoes, cars, and home furnishings. Instead of buying humongous homes, have reasonably-sized ones. Stop buying single-use plastics. Stop dumping chemicals and garbage into the rivers and oceans. Stop depleting the freshwater resources by eating less meat and moving to more plant-based foods.

A major restructuring of taxation is direly needed, one that keeps the incentives for innovation yet provides an equitable distribution of wealth. The bottom 80 percent would see a rise in their quality of living, while the top 20 percent would see an acceptable decline they would happily favor in the light of the alternative proposition of losing the boat itself; that is, essentially making the world uninhabitable if rapid degradation of the environment is permitted.

So, essentially, yes, we can afford not to grow at the high pace desired. In fact, we need to manage a mandated reduction in growth, to make sure that it is sustainable in the long run.

## Individuals Can Have Substantial Say

Consider the environmental impact of a pair of shoes. It emits the equivalent of 14 kg of carbon dioxide and requires 2,257 gallons of water. It will eventually end up in a landfill and decompose and leach out harmful chemicals into the soil and underground water. More than 20 billion shoes are manufactured every year, and 300 million are discarded, which will take 30 to 40 years to decompose [40].

Examples of water resources required for various items are given in Table 1. [37] [41] [42] :

| Item | Unit | No of items or unit | Gallons of water consumed |
|---|---|---|---|
| Shirt | Gallons | 1 | 400 |
| Car | Gallons | 1 | 39,090 |
| Pair of jeans | Gallons | 1 | 1,899 |
| Board of Lumber | Gallons | 1 | 4 |
| Latte | Cup | 1 | 53 |
| Bottled water | Bottle | 1 | 2 |
| Steel | Ton | 1 | 62,000 |
| Cement | Ton | 1 | 1,360 |
| Wool | Pound | 1 | 101 |
| Cotton | Pound | 1 | 101 |
| Plastic | Pound | 1 | 24 |
| Synthetic Rubber | Pound | 1 | 55 |

| | | | |
|---|---|---|---|
| Lettuce | Pound | 1 | 15 |
| Tomatoes | Pound | 1 | 22 |
| Cabbage | Pound | 1 | 24 |
| Cucumber | Pound | 1 | 28 |
| Potatoes | Pound | 1 | 34 |
| Oranges | Pound | 1 | 55 |
| Apples | Pound | 1 | 83 |
| Bananas | Pound | 1 | 102 |
| Corn | Pound | 1 | 107 |
| Peaches or Nectarines | Pound | 1 | 142 |
| Wheat bread | N/A | 1 | 154 |
| Avocadoes | N/A | 1 | 60 |
| Tofu | Pound | 1 | 302 |
| Rice | Pound | 1 | 449 |
| Olives | Pound | 1 | 361 |
| Chocolate | Pound | 1 | 3,170 |
| Eggs | N/A | 12 | 636 |
| Chicken | Pound | 1 | 518 |
| Cheese | Pound | 1 | 896 |
| Pork | Pound | 1 | 718 |
| Butter | Pound | 1 | 2,044 |
| Beef | Pound | 1 | 1,799 |
| Tea | Oz | 8 | 7 |
| Coffee | Oz | 8 | 29 |
| Wine | Oz | 8 | 58 |

Table 1. Water required to produce various consumables

Per-capita energy use in countries of extreme poverty (individuals earning $1.90/day) is about 10,000 kilowatts per hour (kWh). In richer countries, the rate is about 10,000 kWh to 70,000 kWh.

Let me give you the energy consumption by world region in terawatts (one trillion watts) per hour (TWh) in 2018, as follows [43]:

Asia Pacific: 69,615 TWh energy consumption with 4.3billion population, which includes the following countries:

China, Japan, South Korea, Australia, India, Singapore, Taiwan, New Zealand, Thailand, and Vietnam

North America, 32,936 TWh energy consumption with 579 million population, which includes the following countries:

USA, Canada, Mexico, Guatemala, Belize, Honduras, El Salvador, Nicaragua, Costa Rica, Panama, Bahamas, Cuba, Jamaica, Haiti, Dominican Republic, St. Kitts and Nevis, Antigua and Barbuda, Dominica, St. Lucia, Barbados, St. Vincent and the Grenadines, Trinidad, and Tobago.

Europe, 23,850 TWh energy consumption with 741 million population, which includes the following countries:

Russia, Germany, United Kingdom, France, Spain, Ukraine, Poland, Romania, Netherlands, Belgium, Czech Republic, Greece, Portugal, Sweden, Hungary, Belarus, Austria, Serbia, Switzerland, Bulgaria, Denmark, Finland, Slovakia, Norway, Ireland, Croatia, Moldova, Bosnia and Herzegovina, Albania, Lithuania, North Macedonia, Slovenia, Latvia, Estonia,

Montenegro, Luxembourg, Malta, Iceland, Andorra, Monaco, Liechtenstein, San Marino, Holy See.

Commonwealth of Independent States (CIS), 10,822 TWh energy consumption with 240 million population, which includes the following countries:

Armenia, Azerbaijan, Belarus, Kazakhstan, Kyrgyzstan, Moldova, Russia, Tajikistan, Uzbekistan.

The Middle East, 10,494 TWh energy consumption with 411 million population, which includes the following countries:

Egypt, Iran, Turkey, Iraq, Saudi Arabia, Yemen, Syria, Jordan, United Arab Emirates, Israel, Lebanon, Palestine, Oman, Kuwait, Qatar, Bahrain

South America, 8,164 TWh energy consumption with 423 million population, which includes the following countries:

Colombia, Venezuela, Ecuador, Peru, Brazil, Argentina, Uruguay, Paraguay, Chile, Suriname, Bolivia, and Guyana.

Africa, 5,367 TWh energy consumption with 1.22 billion population, which includes the following countries:

Algeria, Angola, Benin, Botswana, Burkina Faso, Burundi, Cabo Verde, Cameroon, Central African Republic, Chad, Comoros, Congo-Democratic Republic of Chad, Comoros, Congo, Côte d'Ivoire, Djibouti, Egypt, Equatorial Guinea, Eritrea, Eswatini (former Swaziland), Ethiopia, Gabon, Gambia, Ghana, Guinea, Guinea-Bissau, Kenya, Lesotho, Liberia, Libya, Madagascar, Malawi, Mali, Mauritania, Mauritius, Mauritius, Morocco,

Mozambique, Namibia, Niger, Nigeria, Rwanda, Sao Tome and Principe, Senegal, Seychelles, Sierra Leone, Somalia, South Africa, South Sudan, Sudan, Tanzania, Togo, Tunisia, Uganda, Zambia, and Zimbabwe. Please see the summary in Table 2.

| Area | TWh consumption | Population, billion | Per capita kWh/year |
|---|---|---|---|
| Asia Pacific | 69.615 | 4.3 | 1.62 |
| North America | 32.936 | 0.579 | 5.69 |
| Europe | 23.85 | 0.741 | 3.22 |
| CIS | 10.822 | 0.24 | 4.51 |
| Middle East | 10.494 | 0.411 | 2.55 |
| South America | 8.164 | 0.423 | 1.93 |
| Africa | 5.367 | 1.22 | 0.44 |
| Total | 161.248 | 7.914 | 19.96 |

Table 2. Energy consumption by various world region [43]

With your knowledge in the tables above, you can make a choice daily as to which products and energy level you want to use, keeping the environmental impact in mind. Individuals can have a decisive impact on the use of water and energy.

# Children Can Achieve More

As we continue our journey to quality education in the slums, we have evidence that we can achieve far more than originally antici- pated. The amazing progress of our preschool children was originally inconceivable when we started six years ago. Now, there is no going back.

Our after-school tutoring to students in Grades 1 to 5 is tremendously popular among parents in the slum communities, not to speak of the children who have benefitted the most in making inroads to the high-performance level in each class. One teacher said that the students who were first in Grades 1 to 5 were all in her classroom. This is an unbelievable feat since only a few years ago, we thought that we would only be fighting against dropout due to child labor.

We have successfully changed the minds of many parents and the communities about child labor, just because their children are doing so well in schools.

There is this indirect benefit that we have never talked about: the impact on adult education through children. When they go back home, children are instrumental in the learning of their parents. Many parents commit to learning basic reading and writing because they are so interested and curious about the progress of their children.

The parents and the community are amazed. They never expected their children would have a shot at the high quality of education, especially not so close to the doorsteps of their homes. These children were expected to be on the streets, possibly never destined to step foot into a classroom. That is no longer true. They are now among the best on the road to academic achievement.

## Successful Process Accomplished Child Education

I have told the story of my journey in the slums of Bangladesh to educate thousands of children who might otherwise not have set foot in a classroom and continue their education. How the organization DoPeace negotiated its approach to gain support from parents, communities, and partner NGOs is an exercise that needs dissecting so the process can be applied on a broader scale in other disadvantaged communities.

When we started six years ago, the task appeared gargantuan to go to the poorest of the poor slum dwellers and entice them to send their small children to the one-room schools in their neighborhood. More than that, we wanted children to continue with higher education. We had concluded that the only way for children to achieve their true potential was through higher education. After all, nature has given them all that is required to achieve this.

This was a moonshot, and we figured that two contradictory items (low-cost and higher quality) needed to come together to accomplish substantial results. Surprisingly, our trials and tribulations resulted in spectacular success. We provided about 60,000 school enrollments in six years, with a quality of education that was on par, and sometimes better, than private schools where middle-class parents brought their children.

One of the major reasons for our success is the essential endeavor we undertook to enlighten the slum communities and the parents about the long-term benefits of education. That is the key we found that unlocked the doorway to a better future.

What does that have to do with the world that is now on the verge of significant conflicts and ready to self-inflict irreversible damages to humanity? Quite a bit, I believe. If we can influence one billion slum dwellers, then that will have a domino effect of self-healing to the rest of about 6.8 billion people in the world. But that will be a Herculean task. How about changing the lives of a few hundred thousand children? If that is difficult, then how about changing only a few thousand at a time? And that is what we are doing, using the DoPeace.org platform.

It is well known that the impact of a critical mass can gather momentum and influence a much larger population. History is replete with such phenomena as it has changed humanity many times. In fact, this is the norm. Only a handful of people, and on many occasions only one, comes forward with radical ideas to change the world.

We can provide a critical mass of poor children a high-quality education, so they are conscious of the environment, human rights, equality of access to the world resources and preservation of Earth from self-inflicting destruction. They will care about all human beings, not only one kind or another. They will implement justice to all and discrimination against none. These poor children will have an appreciation and gratitude as they were cared for when they were vulnerable. So, by their instinct, they will give back to society and spread good deeds for all.

Let us look at a simplified risk assessment model. We can assess risk as the catastrophic event multiplied with the consequences.

Risk = catastrophic event x consequence.

The catastrophic event here is leaving, say half a billion to one billion children, uneducated. What are the consequences in terms of lost opportunities? The children will grow up lacking the basic skills essential for a productive living—reading, writing, and arithmetic. With minimal knowledge, they will be a target for exploitation. Some of them could be persuaded to do harmful activities. They will be unlikely to realize their potential or contribute to the well-being of the community. Many of them could be a burden on the community. What is the consequence of leaving a child uneducated? Let us define the consequence as:

Consequences of lack of education = lifetime of lost wages (1) + law enforcement cost (2) + cost due to exploitation (3) + lost opportunity of contribution to the community (4) + healthcare cost of neglect and malnutrition (5) + child marriage for girls*

(6) + higher population growth (7) + poor decision-making (8) + shorter lifespan (9)

I have put some sample cost in US dollars in the above equation:

Consequence of lack of education of one child (US dollars): $25,000 (1) + $2,500 (2) + $10,000 (3) + $5,000 (4) + $5,000 (5) + $5,000* (6) + $5,000 (7) + $5,000 (8) + $10,000 (9) = $72,500

*$5,000 is considering average of only 50 percent of population of females.

If we consider a population of one billion children as uneducated, the minimum negative impact will be about $72 trillion, which is quite nominal for the developing nations. I believe that the true figure will be 10 to 100 times more expensive globally. The world GDP was $80 trillion in 2017; half of that—$40 trillion —is from the emerging economies.

Thus, the risk of total lost revenue in the developing world due to not educating children is at least equal to their GDP (if I reduce the lost revenue to only $40 trillion), or perhaps much greater.

I will discuss the cost of educating children using the DoPeace model and its significant impact on the GDP of poor economies later.

## The Life and Work of Ayesha Akter

To determine why we have succeeded, it will be instructive to understand our DoPeace staff. It will be illustrative to give you the profile of one person (out of about 100 in our organization),

Ms. Ayesha Akter, the likes of her are difficult to find. Her accomplishments at DoPeace are stunning. She has a unique academic background combined with superb skills to bring out the best in people. Her calm demeanor, ready smile, respectful mannerism, and commanding presence will draw your attention quickly.

Ayesha supervises DoPeace's eight school system run by our NGO partner called DCPUK, in Rangpur, Bangladesh. She was promoted to this position after teaching the after-school classes.

She exudes a deep understanding of children and the slum communities we serve. The empathy for children shows in all her actions. She addresses each of her 1,850 students by name. How she can manage to remember that is beyond my understanding. She also knows the family background of each student.

She knows the weak areas of each student and gives a schedule to the teacher for their improvement. Then, she will round up a set of weak students in a room and check on their progress. Next, she will provide feedback to the teachers.

She is quite capable of pursuing hard discussions with a teacher if the student's performance does not improve per the agreed-upon plan. This is possible because of the excellent rapport she maintains with the teachers. Nothing is personal, and she makes it clear that her eight centers must achieve excellence.

She claims that the quality of education she has achieved for our preschools are better than a chain of known schools for well-to-do parents. She also has this policy to allow admission to students belonging to middle-class families who are convinced of the standard of the school, but only two or three of them. This way, our children and the community will have this validation that the school is on par with other name brand schools.

Ayesha has developed strong ties with the parents and the community. She has a reputation in the community that is enviable—the parents will gravitate around her as she visits her schools and discusses their children.

The other day, a journalist showed up at one of her classrooms, and after observing the class, he was quite upset. He declared that the teachers are covering far more material than necessary and subjecting the minds of the students with undue stress that will be harmful! He threatened to publish his negative review in the newspaper. This created quite a bit of back and forth with the class instructor; they informed Ayesha, who immediately decided to visit the classroom. In the meantime, the parents and several other community members showed up and vigorously argued against him. Finally, the journalist capitulated and apologized to Ayesha.

The comradery she has developed with the community members, teachers, and students is instrumental in creating a brand for her schools. She has no problem attracting students to her centers and also admitting the graduates to class one in primary schools.

She has all 30 students in each of her centers appear in the ongoing fifth grade Primary School Certificate (PSC) national exams, a total of 240 students and believes that all of them will get an A grade and many A-pluses.

## The Looming Danger of Leaving Behind the Disadvantaged

I am in favor of progress, innovation, and discovery to find our place on Earth and in the universe—not that it matters if I, or anyone else, is not in favor. My contention—as I have articulated before—is that we are moving without regard to the negative and dangerous aspects of the momentum that is consuming us.

The negative aspects are snowballing and have the possibility of simply undermining our progress and ultimately reversing it, leading to rather primitive living. This is perhaps a dramatic prognosis, aired by many, but it has a strong rationale to it.

It stems from the very human nature hardwired in the brain over millions of years of evolution. It is the fear of harm or demise that triggers the worst in us. We have a strong urge to defend and preserve ourselves, mostly from perceived and imagined threats. In this zeal, we will build an army, amass the most destructive weapons, go to war, occupy land and property, carry guns, live behind triple-locked doors, and won't allow our children to meet with any strangers.

Out of 4.5 billion years of Earth's existence, modern humans have existed here for only 200 to 300 thousand years. Recorded history is only about 5,000 years old. The first radio came in 1894, and the first digital computer in 1940.

In this remarkably minuscule span of time, we have managed to create weapons of mass destruction that can annihilate us many times over.

If we just set aside any violent destruction due to the use of weapons of mass destruction in our discussion, simply ignoring a largely disadvantaged population in the long run, will be upsetting enough to destabilize peace on earth. The friction created by a few who will be grabbing the planet's major resources, leaving the rest behind, maybe harmful enough.

However, there are other ways to live that have the promise to avoid any catastrophic effects. We need to revise our mindset that self-preservation built into our psyche should not supersede the rational mind. We need to distinguish between the actual and the perceived threat so we do not overreact or overreach to harm others.

The rational thing to do is to bring the disadvantaged and the poor along through education and resource allocation. The investment is relatively low, and the return on investment is remarkably high. It surely beats the chaos created by disregarding a significant population and leaving them with their own meager resources. Even worse would be leaving them to the mercy of those who will exploit them to harm us all.

## Our Child Development Approaches

Massive research continues on the topic of child development. DoPeace and its partners address this problem on several fronts. The first one is the most important one. We convince the parents and the community that the child should be in a classroom and not on the streets. This is not so straightforward, and I have discussed this at length in the past and in my book published last year, entitled *Under the Starry Nights*. Over the past six years, we have successfully accomplished this within the communities we serve.

Second, we have a safe place for children ages 4 to 12. They are under the care of our teachers who give them unprecedented love and affection, so they cannot wait to come back. This is a critical part of child development.

Third, as our teachers treat children with utter respect, the children return the same respect to the teachers. We believe that mutual respect is a vital element of child development.

Fourth, we are totally transparent, with our classrooms right in the middle of the community where the parents can observe the ongoing classroom activities if they like. This has built trust and we are able to leverage this trust to ask the parents to make hard decisions; the most important one is to forego child labor and let children continue with their education.

Fifth, we create dreams as children participate in the daily Pledge. They are quite excited about their positive future, as are their parents and the community.

Sixth, our high standard of education gives them the cognitive abilities to help them make better decisions as they move forward.

We are quite cognizant of our children's development and work to make sure they will become contributing members of the future generation.

## Back to Dhaka and Ready to Work

November 16, 2019. I was back in Bangladesh. Despite the low cost of operation, the quality of education was increased gradually to the point that our students now have guaranteed admission in government and private primary schools. Our after-school program has produced tremendous results in retaining children in school and improving their grades. The fifth-grade results of our students in the national PSC exams show a remarkably high pass rate.

Our earliest students are in eleventh grade. I have provided the projection for the next 5, 10, and 15 years in my first book, showing the possibilities as we continue our operations.

We are not complacent or basking on in our success. In fact, this is the beginning, and we have a long way to go. There are about half a million children under the age of five the world over who can use our model to get into the educational system.

We are vigilant; we are active; and we have a laser focus on our mission. Disadvantaged and poor children have the right to an education, and we will continue to do our part.

## Educating Children in Extreme Poverty

Twenty-six percent of the world's population are very young, 15 years or less, but the older population, 65 years or more, is only

9 percent [44]. The European population is much older, about 20 percent are 65 or up [45]. Keep in mind the dramatic growth rate of the world's population: one billion in 1800, 6 billion in 2000, 7.7 billion in 2019, projected to be 8.5 billion in 2030, and 11 billion in 2100 [46].

A whopping 1.4 billion live below the poverty line, and 591 million live in extreme poverty. Data on some of the major countries are listed in Table 3.

| Country | Millions below poverty line | Country | Millions below poverty line | Country | Millions below poverty line |
|---|---|---|---|---|---|
| India | 299 | China | 47 | Philippines | 23 |
| Nigeria | 140 | Bangladesh | 39 | Afghanistan | 20 |
| Pakistan | 63 | Ethiopia | 33 | Japan | 20 |
| Mexico | 58 | Indonesia | 29 | Russia | 19 |
| Congo, Democratic Republic of | 64 | Egypt | 27 | Kenya | 19 |
| U.S.A. | 49 | Sudan | 25 | Madagascar | 19 |
| Nigeria | 95 | Uganda | 16 | Malawi | 13 |
| Ethiopia | 26 | Afghanistan | 16 | Venezuela | 12 |
| Tanzania | 22 | Mozambique | 15 | South Sudan | 10 |
| Madagascar | 20 | Niger | 13 | Indonesia | 9 |
| Yemen | 18 | South Africa | 13 | Zambia | 9 |
| Myanmar | 14 | Sudan | 13 | Brazil | 9 |

Table 3. Some countries with the largest population below the poverty line. About 1.4 billion live below the poverty line, and 591 million live in extreme poverty (income $1.90 per day or below). Derived from [47] [48] [110].

As you know, one of my main goals is to educate the poorest of the poor children. I have discussed at length the reasons why I feel strongly about this in my previous book. Early childhood education is one of the key factors that impact the growth of a man or a woman and sets the stage for future development. I see poverty as strongly related to education. The less educated the person is, the less he or she has in earning potential. Conversely, education leads to higher income. I have witnessed the perpetual cycle of poverty in the slums, and it is caused by generations who remain practically illiterate.

Tables 3 and 4 provide the landscape of the levels of poverty in various countries. I presume that long-term poverty reduction is not possible without providing early childhood education in poor countries. About 300 million children 0 to 14 years of age are in poverty as shown in Table 4.

| **Country** | **Millions of children 0 to 14 in poverty** | **Country** | **Millions of children 0-14 in poverty** | **Country** | **Millions of children 0 to 14 in poverty** |
|---|---|---|---|---|---|
| India | 80.77 | China | 8.52 | Philippines | 7.23 |
| Nigeria | 61.91 | Bangladesh | 11.09 | Afghanistan | 8.91 |
| Pakistan | 22.30 | Ethiopia | 13.59 | Japan | 2.66 |
| Mexico | 15.92 | Indonesia | 7.96 | Russia | 3.49 |
| Congo, Democratic Republic of | 22.49 | Egypt | 9.45 | Kenya | 7.65 |

| | | | | | |
|---|---|---|---|---|---|
| United States of America | 9.44 | Sudan | 10.30 | Madagascar | 7.83 |

Table 4. Children 0 to 14 years of age in poverty, a total of about 300 million [49] [50].

Out of the total poor population of the world, half are extremely poor—that is, they live on $1.90 a day. This is one of the most significant problems facing the Earth.

## Why is Educating Poor Children Critical?

Poverty is pivotal to many critical elements that impact the world, among them high birth rates, health concerns, crimes, low quality of life, short lifespans, political unrest, and illiteracy. Poor countries have high birth rates [51]; the larger the population of children, the fewer resources are available for their well-being. The most important impact is on their education. We notice the lack of emphasis on primary education in poor countries, and this has a far-reaching impact. The children not having primary education are unlikely to catch up later when they are a little bit older. There are some programs for the education of older children, but they are not enough.

One big reason why developing nations are not able to dodge poverty is because a large proportion of the population is not adequately educated. In fact, the lack of primary (and higher) education is the main cause that a country remains a poor nation with rampant poverty [52]. Developing nations have not emphasized primary education as a critical element for the development of the country over the long-term. Since developing a nation requires a rather long-term strategy, it escapes the radar of poor nations as they generally deal with short-term economic woes.

Poor countries tend to have leadership honing in on short-term progress. The political structure may not allow for developing the educational infrastructure on solid ground. In many cases, the poor countries have a predominantly lopsided economy (perhaps not too different from some advanced economies). The small, rich population has school availability for their children based on the private enterprise that caters to them. On the flip side, the poor are in an overwhelming majority, devoid of adequate government-run schools that can provide quality education.

In many places, the government has forsaken the poor children and given up on their education, even when laws are written to provide primary education to all children. In some countries, NGOs are doing a remarkable job of providing primary education at little or no cost to the children. However, by definition, third parties cannot do the job of the government who is obligated to provide primary education to the millions and millions of children in the nation.

I have discussed an approach that DoPeace, an NGO registered in Pennsylvania, USA, has taken to provide preschool education to children four-and-a-half to six years old and move them to primary schools. The remarkable part of this approach is that it is done at the incredibly low cost of one US dollar per month per child. This low-cost yet high-quality education is a solution to the education of children in extreme poverty.

I have used this approach to educate the poor children in the slums of Bangladesh and Pakistan, as well as inner-city children in Philadelphia, USA, which is in the initial stages. This system is proven viable and has resulted in more than 60,000 school enrollments in Bangladesh in the last six years.

## About 300 Million Children in Extreme Poverty Are at Risk

According to the World Clock, there are about 600 million people in the world under extreme poverty of earnings below $1.90 per day, some of which are countries depicted in Table 2. In these poor countries, 50 percent of the population consists of children, thus there are about 300 million children in poverty [53]. All of them are exposed to the risk of either never entering primary school or dropping out if they do enter. I must also mention that almost half of the young children in the United States live in poverty or near poverty [54].

The current approach to early childhood and primary education is based on the remarkably high cost of infrastructure development. It entails, primarily, the development of school buildings first. The budget of such construction for a million children could easily be $100 to $150 per child; that is $100 to $150 million when added together. The yearly expenses of running the school would be half that cost, so $50 to $75 million. This is punitive for a country like Madagascar with 7.8 million children, which costs some $780 million in infrastructure and $370 million in yearly expenses, where the average income is $2.20 per day per person.

Thus, a developing or poor country would not be able to afford early childhood or primary school education, and thus sustained poverty continues for generations.

The only solution is to adopt a low-cost model of education, as opposed to the traditional, high capital intensive model. Thus, DoPeace's low-cost model, or any other similar model, at the total expense of one US dollar per month per child, is the only viable solution available. This model beats waiting years for the money to arrive, or worse, thinking that early childhood or primary school education can be given a low priority.

# When Pandemic Strikes

When a particularly virulent pandemic strikes, the results could be devastating, infecting, and killing millions of humans within weeks. This is what occurred when I started writing about the topic in January 2019, and soon the novel coronavirus struck. Now, it is on its way to kill more than a million people before an effective vaccine or medicine that takes us out of our current misery.

At the time of writing this book, FDA in the USA has approved the Pfizer and BioNTech vaccine on December 12, 2020, that is reported as 95 percent effective. UK has already approved the same vaccine on December 2, 2020.

The HIV/AIDS pandemic killed 32 million people by 2005 (the world population was 6.5 billion at the time). The Hong Kong flu killed one million in 1968 (the world population was 3.5 billion). Asian flu killed two million from 1956 to 1958 (world population was 2.8 billion). The Spanish flu pandemic from 1918 to 1920 killed 50 million (world population was 1.8 billion). The sixth cholera pandemic of 1910 and 1911 killed about a million (world population was 1.6 billion). The Russian flu of 1889 and 1890 killed one million (world population was 1.6 billion). The third cholera pandemic from 1852 to 1860 killed ten million (world population was 1.2 billion). The Black Death or bubonic plague from 1346 to 1353 killed 25 million (world population was 350 million). The Plague of Justinian in 541 and 542 killed 25 to 50 million (world population was 200 million). The Antonine Plague, a typhoid outbreak, of 165 to 180 AD killed 5 million (world population was 190 million). [55]

In earlier periods, the only means of spreading a virus or bacteria across the continents was through sea transportation. It was relatively slower to spread deadly diseases across continents. Now, it is super easy to travel from one continent to another through air travel—with about 100,000 flights and 12 million passengers flying per day [56].

A new strain of the virus is generally transported to a human in a remote location from an animal, which is the source. Previous sources of the virus have been birds, pigs, bats, horses, dogs, and humans. A hybrid between animal and human viruses can create a deadly new virus. It could be from other sources, or mutations of the existing viruses for which the development of vaccines may not be produced after a short timeframe. Humans may not have immunity to a new strain of the virus. Thus, the virus moves rapidly and exponentially because it spreads through contact or droplets in the air.

Pandemics are a real threat in modern times and has the potential to kill up to 80 million people. Our response is mostly reactive as the threat looms. Climate change exacerbates the spread of viruses and microbes due to increasing heat and humidity.

This causes a change in the pattern of migration of birds and animals, and the new breed of viruses spread by mosquitoes. The disease can be propagated within weeks to billions with no immunity.

Even when research is being pursued to develop generic vaccines against a host of viruses, the effort is far less intense than warranted, and the time may be running out before the next set of deadly diseases (post-COVID-19) strike and paralyze a large population.

COVID-19 has changed the way we live and interact with our community within months of its appearance. It is said that the world will not be the same again. We will be in constant threat of contagious viruses, one after another. We will keep inventing vaccines and drugs to combat them. We will get accustomed to a new normal. The impact will be long-term and insidious. Whether the world will be better or worse—economically and socially—depends on what the citizens of the world will allow, and what the tyrants can get away with. We are at the crossroads of a historical choice.

## Coronavirus: A Manifestation of Growth

The spread of the novel coronavirus illustrates how easy it is to transmit unknown viruses from animals to humans, and this is the manifestation of rapid growth resulting in the shrinking distance between animals and humans. The hundreds of thousands of viruses that have been lurking in the depth of the jungles are now close to humans due to fast deforestation and human consumption, according to Katrina Zimmer (National Geographic, Nov. 22, 2019).

Technology and better infrastructure help to produce more, create more jobs, allow for more disposable income, and gives the ability to buy more. This further allows for better technology and more efficiency. Thus, the cycle of growth is on upswing over the long haul, just like the stock market that keeps increasing the average over a long period.

The problem is that the more dependent we are on technology and higher efficiency, the more work we have created for ourselves, as we need to keep going just to keep pace with the monster we created. We may have more stuff, but we are more stressed and less joyful. An overwhelming majority of the world population is barely making it and are in survival mode. This is simply the flawed system they are a part of—with or without their consent.

However, we are all exposed to the pandemic, rich or poor. The rich have a much bigger role in its creation since they are the ones who dominate the managerial decision-making of companies who drive consumption, including deforestation. But most of the consequences from the creation and spread of the virus will fall on 80 percent of the world's population, which are poorer.

The pattern linking growth and the devastating spread of the pandemic is quite known:

Growth >> higher consumption >> deforestation >> closer contact with animals with viruses >> pandemic >> fast spread and high fatalities among the poor (as well as rich, but they have lower numbers).

## Beyond COVID-19

"We hold these truths to be self-evident, that all men are created equal, that they are endowed by their Creator with certain unalienable Rights, that among these are Life, Liberty and the pursuit of Happiness."

These are the words written by Thomas Jefferson in The Declaration of Independence. They have reverberated in the hearts and minds of people in the USA and all around the world for the last 244 years. The American experiment gave rise to American Exceptionalism, as America successfully changed the world forever. America, the longest continuously held government in the history of the world, has been the cornerstone for democracy and liberation, a melting pot that exists nowhere, where liberated women are able to live independently, and where everyone has the freedom to worship whomever they choose. America gave us electric light, sewing machines, telegraphs, telephones, cars, airplanes, personal computers, and mobile phones. Heck, even ice cream was invented here. You may be wondering what the rest of the world was doing in the meantime.

What the world was doing was changing, physically and conceptually, and recent events do not coincide with so much enthusiasm for what I will call the Second American Experiment. This experiment has given stark inequality, inconsistent with what uplifted the country and the world in the last 200 years. The pursuit of happiness has turned into the pursuit of wealth, absent of happiness, and has divided the country as never before. Politics are one of the biggest divisions among citizens. The laws are rigged for mega multinational businesses that are too big to fail. They are virtual monopolies, with little regard to the environment—the same environmental damage that is ready to devour us soon.

The operating word of the Second American Experiment is consumption, the ever-increasing rate of consumption. Consumption rules everything, and it is the economic engine of the world. Absent the increasing rate of consumption, the stock market will plunge, for starters; consequently, there will be no money available for businesses to expand, or seed money for entrepreneurs. The MBAs will see decreased opportunities. There will be no traction for businesses to sell their hardware or services all over the world. The question is why the rate of consumption will ever decrease to trigger all the bad things I just said.

Good question, and there could be several reasons, but we see one already. COVID-19 is not an entirely new phenomenon in the history of pandemics, but a different one in our lifetime perhaps. Consumption and production are substantially reduced, and the stock market is uncertain. I am sure this will pass, and I hope without intolerable harm. But what happens if future pandemics become more frequent and even more deadly? What happens if there is nuclear warfare? Consider environmental damage so major, metropolitan cities are underwater. What if the major supply chain is disrupted, and we cannot access our medicine or other essentials? What happens if the dictators, monarchs, rouge heads of states, and military chiefs go berserk and kill millions of their subjects?

You may think that these doomsday scenarios are farfetched, and I hope they are. COVID-19 was farfetched just a few months ago. But I think the world has changed in a blink and our lives will not be the same again. There is a saying that misfortune does not come alone, and we must guard against that.

The rampant rise in consumption must be reduced so the world can be sustained. Environmental damage must be controlled. Nuclear warheads must be abolished. Economic inequities must be leveled. Big businesses must be kept under control.

Is the world ready for a new economic system, equitable living standards, and collaboration rather than confrontation? Can the USA lead again?

## COVID-19: The Implications

What I had been writing prior to the debacle of COVID-19, which was not too long ago, has come to a head in such a stark way.

I have been arguing about slowing down consumption, stop big business from complete immunity from its reckless profit-making, disrupt globalization that big businesses thrive on, and subject local small businesses from the vicious competition from the virtual monopolies. And change laws to break the power of big businesses.

Further, I would like to see the ability of the system to create billionaires to stop. Currently, the combined wealth of only eight people is more than the combined wealth of the lower half of the world population [8], and that is unconscionable. Further, 71 percent of the world's population lives on less than $10 per day [57], and 50 percent less than $5.50 per day [15]. In 2015 (the latest estimates available), 10 percent of the world's population lived in extreme poverty (less than $1.90 a day) [53]. The entire health budget of Ethiopia, a country of 105 million people, is equivalent to just 1 percent of the fortune of the world's richest man, Amazon CEO Jeff Bezos [15].

It is justifiable to halt the economic system against the accumulation of obscene wealth. Arguably, the utility of a few becoming super-rich and their contribution to the well-being of people are quite exaggerated.

COVID-19 produced a dip in the economic engine, with consumption dropping sharply. Shops all over the world are closed or operating at low capacity, which is a stark departure from business as usual. What happens after this economic slowdown has yet to be seen. In the meantime, the world is under quarantine as never imagined in recent history. Human misery is stark on a global scale.

The effect of lockdown meant fewer vehicles on the road and little air travel. The positive impact on environmental pollution cannot be ignored. Air pollution has been an ongoing trauma on the health of children and older people and causes a significant number of premature deaths. It is rumored that the reduction of death due to poor air quality is as high as the deaths caused by COVID-19, but it remains to be seen if that is the case. It is known that air pollution kills many more people than HIV/AIDS, malaria, alcohol consumption, and drug abuse. The environmental impact reduces the life expectancy of the global population by about three years.

If we do notice a significantly better environmental condition, even if it is temporary for the duration of lockdown, there are lessons to be learned. I am hoping human behavior will be modified as we come out of this pandemic, and this will be a precursor to significantly improved conditions, saving many more lives.

## COVID-19: A Test Case

In many respects, this pandemic rips apart all the artificial façades and makes bare our true selves. Who we are as human beings is determined by what we believe in and how we treat others. Do we revere our interests above and beyond the needs of others? Further, are we smart enough to see that we are all in this together? This is true not only for this pandemic, but for all the impending disasters we have been inadvertently planning for years. That includes nuclear war, environmental debacles, biological and chemical warfare, artificial intelligence, and gene drive. And not least, the future pandemics that could be more frequent and deadly.

I have heard the unproven theory that in the universe, there may be millions or billions of Earth-like planets that are teeming with life. Smart lives evolve everywhere. Unfortunately, these entities are self-destructive. Within about 10,000 years of existence as intelligent life, they run beyond their wits and destroy themselves. These experiments are naturally occurring throughout the universe, but perhaps not one of them has dodged self-destruction. This theory may be total fiction, but it is within the realm of plausibility. That is why many, including ground-breaking physicist Steven Hawking, implored us to spread out to other planets to save humanity.

We have no choice but to find a solution to the impulse of self-destruction. The main problem, as I see it, is all of these separate countries we have created are ready and willing to indulge in senseless endeavors, at least periodically. These countries are governed by, in most places, powerful elites, who control decision-making for their own benefit, and at the expense of their fellow citizens, and to the citizens of the world.

Long-term rational decision-making has not been prevalent historically. The interest of a country, in most cases, will be limited to its boundaries; and for the elites dominating the country and their cronies. The impact is global, as we are witnessing in this pandemic, and we are all stakeholders in a decision made anywhere in the world.

In the past, countries were taken out of the control of kings, at great sacrifices. Now, there is no appetite to go over the borders to stop the elites from harming their own citizens. The main reason is that true democracy by the people and for the people exists in limited countries. And even those countries elect their representatives to govern for several years, and for all those years, all bets are practically off. The elected officials are free to make senseless decisions, which can hurt their people and others across the border, with virtually no restrictions.

The reaction of various countries to tackle the pandemic is an indicator that each one is acting on its own. In most countries, there is no unified, intelligent, and consistent effort to combat the disease. The constraints of available resources are ubiquitous, even in rich countries. Poor countries are no match for the challenge, and are waiting to face the impending disaster on their own. Deaths of two to three million people are eminent, either quite quickly within months or in a prolonged period over a year or two before the pandemic is over.

Anyone can see that this pandemic should be handled by the unified and concerted efforts of the united world. That has not happened. That speaks volumes about the fractured world that we live in. Unless the world is truly united, we are not using our full capability. This pandemic is simply the test case of our ability to prepare and handle the future, perhaps even as deadlier disasters are waiting to come our way.

## Children During the COVID-19 Lockdown

COVID-19 has put educational efforts in Bangladesh and Karachi on hold, like many other places. About 10,000 children in DoPeace are homebound. These children are residents of slums and are the poorest of the poor. The parents are most likely going without a livelihood, living under duress, as if the normal daily manual labor were not enough hardship for them.

Schools in many countries have switched to online learning. Parents are home and helping in their children's education. That is not possible in the homes of children in slums. The parents there are mostly illiterate.

By design, our curriculum is quite intense and our students have responded by doing remarkably well. I have gone into quite a bit of detail about our program in the book, *Under the Starry Nights*. At this time there are several quite ambitious initiatives taking place that will upscale children's education to the next level. However, the schedule of such actions is uncertain. COVID-19 will determine when we will start working with full force.

## Impact of COVID-19 on Preschool Education

As you know, DoPeace has about 10,000 children studying in Bangladesh, from preschool to the fifth grade, and their education has been interrupted since the middle of March 2020. They have been instructed to stay at home and maintain social distancing as much as they can. The impact on their learning for several months has been devastating. Our preschool education is very fast-paced, and 4.5 to 5 years old children cover 70 percent of the 1st-grade curriculum in one year. This has been designed to provide the children in the slums a competitive edge over the children growing up in the families outside the slums. The educational model and the strategy have produced staggering results, with a dropout of less than 5 percent, and higher performance year after year.

Now with COVID-19 and a setback of several months, we are planning a lot of catchups. We opened schools from June 1, 2020, but it is drastically scaled-down, with only ten students in the classroom at any time. Students wash their hands before entering the classroom, wear masks, and follow social distancing.

Bangladesh had 420,238 infections and total deaths of 6,067 as of November 8, 2020, with a country of 161 million, which is 3.77 deaths per 100,000 population. In comparison, deaths per 100,000 population for Belgium is 113; the United Kingdom, 73.66; Spain, 83.11; Italy, 67.95; and the United States, 72.42 [58]. Bangladesh is far below the COVID-19 risk, but there is no guarantee that the infection will not spread in the future, so its residents cannot be too complacent. However, we believe that from the risk and/or benefit of children's education versus no education, the benefit of restarting education far outweighs the risk in Bangladesh. The decision to start educating children must be made on a country by country basis, depending on the risk environment.

The problems in handling education in this pandemic are quite different for children in the slums versus the rest of the world. Most developing nations are turning to online learning as a solution. Even there, the low-income and minority populations are suffering as they have difficulty adapting. First, internet resources and learning platforms may not be equally available for the poorer population. Second, the parents are most likely uneducated or unskilled to help children in the transition to online learning. Third, struggling poor parents looking for income are far more stressed about their job situation, rather than the education of their children, which must take a back-seat for now.

In the slums, we have the same situation of parents seeking income. However, we never relied on parents taking an active part in educating their children, as we have designed our educational system to compensate for the rather scant education of parents.

Our teachers, supervisors, and executive directors are quite excited to resume educational activities and compensate for lost education. This will be slow at first, as we need to learn and adapt to the pandemic.

Our whole organization of about 100 staff members is ready to take on the challenge and do what we have been doing for the last six years—educate the disadvantaged.

## The World Taken Hostage by a Virus

Although it was predictable, the ferocity of the COVID-19 spread has still overtaken all. We are homebound and in retreat. It is difficult to capture how much the world has changed so swiftly. We can all stay at home, for a long period of time, to keep our families and us safe, but how will we live without wages?

Rich countries can provide some relief, poor ones cannot do much. I have said it many times to bring it home, 71 percent of the world lives on $10 per day or less [57], and 50 percent on $2.50 per day [15]. So, there is serious vulnerability here. A huge population will face malnutrition soon, living with perhaps on one meal a day, and even starvation.

There is a race for medicine or vaccine, but until that happens, hardship will take hold for the poor and most vulnerable first. No one knows how long it will take for an effective vaccine to be available for the world, and particularly those who will be on the edge of the precipice.

Even when the virus is a great equalizer, it is opportunistic. It thrives on the path of least resistance—the uneducated, unprepared, and poor—many with no choice but to be on the front line. The impact due to the dichotomy of the world—with 20 percent (at best) as the well to do and the rest as an underclass—is showing to some extent now. But it is possible that we will see this in starker terms soon.

There are some poor nations in South Asia and Africa that may have dodged the bullet, rather surprisingly, and without a full explanation. I just hope that remains to be the case; the health system there is well known to be ill-equipped to handle a potential disaster. Even the healthcare system in New York State has been found to be severely lacking, and this is supposedly a rich territory. Dead bodies have been everywhere in New York, some stacked in body bags, and in the queue for cremation, with no proper ceremony, as loved ones are not allowed or are unwilling to come anywhere near them.

The U.S. has borne the brunt of this pandemic, and the world is aghast at its unpreparedness. Seemingly, the population has adjusted or is already exhausted to this grim drama that is unfolding every day. There seems to be some resignation to fate. Statistics are used to show how only less than 2.6 percent of the population who are infected suffer a fatality. There is no overwhelming outrage that I expect at the sheer number of dead in such a short period of time, as the body count is growing daily. This shows that human beings can adapt to the most severe conditions in a relatively short period of time, creating perhaps an inconceivable new normal.

In the meantime, we are praying for effective drugs and vaccines, as masks and social distancing can work only so much in the long run.

## COVID-19 and Hunger

Fear has gripped us all in the face of the pandemic. Ultimately, it is the fear of death, but the fear of loss of livelihood drives all of us until we fall victim to the novel coronavirus. How would we feed ourselves and our families in the meantime? The ones in real danger are those not reading this because they are not able to read. On one side are those who can read and write and perhaps can feed themselves. Then there are others—the ones who cannot read and write as much, are poor, and struggle to survive. They have no representation and live in a parallel world without really participating in it.

There are plenty of people like me who may write about them but do not really understand them. We pretend to understand their pain and suffering, but we really do not. We get some comfort in writing about them, perhaps out of guilt, or perhaps showing that we are morally better. But it does not make any difference.

I got sidetracked a little bit. Let me get back to the numbers—not just any number, but the number of deaths every year around the world and the causes of death, as shown in Table 5.

| **Causes of deaths by risk factor** | **Global Deaths, 2017** |
|---|---|
| Blood pressure | 10,440,818 |
| Hunger | 9,000,000 |
| Blood sugar | 6,526,028 |
| Smoking | 7,099,111 |
| Air pollution (outdoor & indoor) | 4,895,476 |
| Obesity | 4,724,346 |
| Outdoor air pollution | 3,408,878 |
| Diet high in sodium | 3,196,514 |
| Diet low in whole grains | 3,065,589 |
| Alcohol use | 2,842,854 |
| Few fruits | 2,423,447 |
| Few nuts and seeds | 2,062,522 |
| Indoor air pollution | 1,640,600 |
| Few vegetables | 1,462,367 |
| Low omega 3 | 1,444,907 |
| Little exercise | 1,263,051 |
| Secondhand smoke | 1,220,044 |
| Birth weight | 1,096,977 |

| | |
|---|---|
| Child wasting | 1,077,102 |
| Unsafe sex | 1,028,620 |
| Low fiber | 873,408 |
| Coronavirus | 1,027,634 |

Table 5. The causes of death per risk factor versus the number of deaths in 2017 [59].

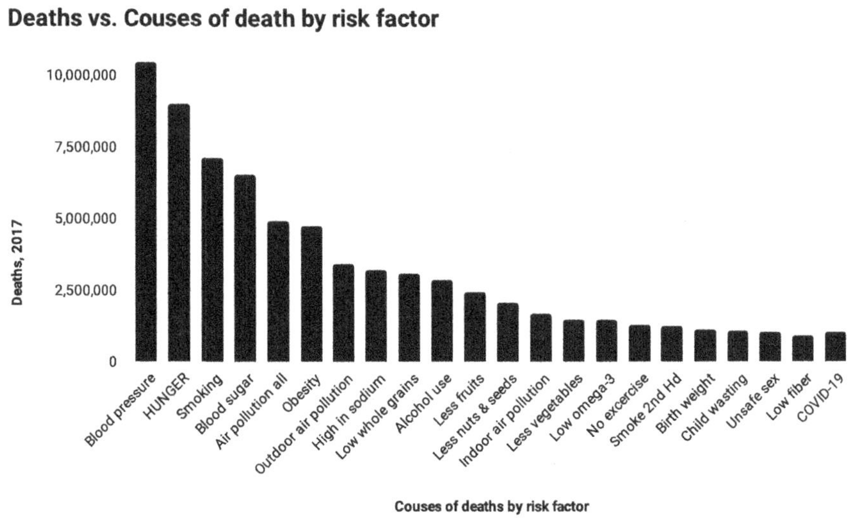


Figure 1. The causes of death per risk factor versus the number of deaths in 2017 [59].

As Table 5 and Figure 1 indicate, the highest death rate is caused by high blood pressure, which accounts for more than 10 million deaths globally. The other causes are smoking (7 million), high blood sugar (6 million), air pollution (5 million), obesity (5 million), high sodium diets (3 million), low sodium diets (3 million)—sodium wise, you don't win either way—diets low in whole grain (3 million), and alcohol use (3 million) are also deadly

The new coronavirus is almost the last in the list, which is predicted to cause about one million deaths in 2020. But one that is most deadly is hunger, which causes 9 million deaths every year, and is slated to be doubled due to COVID-19. That could be about 18 million deaths due to hunger, and that pales in comparison to any cause of death in recent history. One reason is that COVID-19 has sapped the means of earning for a significant portion of the poor.

That is what we are dealing with. Now, I have burned the midnight oil thinking about it, but I am not hungry. I agonize, but I do not really know how it feels to die of hunger. I just dread thinking about it and wonder why the world is like that.

## The Minimalist in the Era of Pandemics

It was never clear as to what it is like to be forced to live without essentials, even when you have money. That is, until now, in the COVID-19 pandemic. Items that people must forgo in developed economies may be different than in developing economies. How much people must let go of their lifestyles is pain that is felt everywhere, but it is not equal in all parts of the world.

With lost wages, the visual of a lineup of cars to get charitable food, in a rich country like the USA, is both heartbreaking and eye-opening. The cost of living for a family of four in New York, is more than $4,000 per month, while the medium income is $4,800 per month [60]. In Dhaka, Bangladesh, they are about $500 and $570, respectively [61] (for comparison, Dhaka is a little more expensive than Kolkata, India). I am comparing two expensive cities, in two contrasting parts of the world. With income and expenses eight times less, it is quite affordable to maintain the status quo of a person in Dhaka, either by help from a relative working in Europe, a neighbor, a donation from an NGO, or the government handout. However, it is difficult to hand out $4,000 per month on a sustained basis in New York. In Bangladesh, the average wages per month are 15,100 BDT [62], which is about $179 USD, much less than that in Dhaka, and overall more affordable.

Thus, the argument goes, a disaster or pandemic will be significantly less devastating in Bangladesh compared to more developed nations, in terms of pure economics.

The essential material possessions, now revealed more starkly in the pandemic, are shelter, food, clean water, hygiene, reasonable clothing, internet, and mobile phones. Of course, you need money to afford all of that.

The rest are non-essentials.

I have worked in the slums of Bangladesh for the last six years, so I am acutely familiar with what are essentials. For slum dwellers, basic subsistence living is their way of life, and they struggle to get that. Humans, of course, strive to achieve far more than the essentials, because it may make life more interesting. However, the pandemic has changed everything.

There are an overwhelming number of people, all over the world, who are content with essentials at this time, to the point that meals are difficult to get, as I have pointed out above. On the other hand, many have money, yet they cannot get everything that money can buy for them. Under the pandemic lockdown, money has limited utility.

If the future holds other pandemics, and this is such a terrible thing to say, then frequent lockdowns are not farfetched, particularly if a new virus appears for which vaccines are not readily available. The cycle can repeat—sickness and suffering, lockdowns, new drugs, new vaccines, then a new normal.

In the era of pandemics, a new economic system is inevitable, which revolves around minimalism—less consumption, environmental preservation, national and international cooperation, better resource utilization, and no wars. People will finally come to the realization that we are all in it together.

Pandemics will teach us that we need to live within our resources and achieve sustainability. Spawning megacities; vanishing forests; melting glaciers; rising sea levels; and stockpiling of atomic, chemical, and biological weapons are counterproductive to our long-term survival on this Earth. I am hoping that we all will become minimalists in the era of pandemics.

## Earth's Message to Humans

Hello, Earthlings. I have seen something strange here. Unexpectedly, you folks are emitting much less pollution; I see much less traffic on the road and in the air. The skies are clearer, as you attest to better visibility in your cities, mountains, and even the night sky is far more illuminated with stars. I have seen your carbon emissions reduce by 7 percent [63] and the nitrogen oxide emission by 30-40 percent in many cities [64].

That seems to be a good move on your part, as that has saved you about 77,000 lives [65] due to this reduction in pollution, particularly those particulates. But do not think I do not know why that has happened, with no credit to you. I know you, and you are not so smart to be able to reduce environmental degradation.

You have been forced to do so. You cannot handle that novel coronavirus. You do not know what to do about it. Your most high-tech device is to hide behind four walls, not mingle with your kind, and wear a mask and keep your distance.

Folks, I know you are preoccupied with the COVID-19 pandemic. Unfortunately, it is on its way to kill about 450,000 in the U.S.A., and 2.7 million globally by March 1, 2021. However, you procreate about 81 million people every year [66]. Since 1800—when the population was only one billion—you have added more than 6 billion in just 220 years. When it comes to procreating, there is no limit to what you can do.

This pandemic is still child's play compared to the last one—the one you called Spanish Flu for some reason—that infected 500 million, one-third of the world population, and killed 50 million, in 1918 and 1919. Then there were several other pandemics. You never learned from previous outbreaks, and you start each time all over again.

Again, I am not fooled by this temporary bounce in environmental revival, as I do not expect you to do any better when choices are given to you. Already I see that your environmental regulations are being relaxed. You have allowed deforesting in the Amazon rainforests, poaching in Africa, slowing the environmental diplomacy, and stopping investment in green energy. I guess that is because your economy is tanking. But you folks did not do much to contain environmental degradation, even when the economy was booming for years.

I am rebounding and flourishing for now, as you are homebound and out of work. The closing of factories, much-reduced transportation, and lower electrical generation is good news for me. But that is not going to last for long. Soon, as always, you will be back to your mischief and polluting at an even faster rate. Me, the Earth, will be back in a defensive position.

# A World Badly in Need of Repair

We now have a world that is quite dysfunctional, because of disparate leadership and ideologies in conflict with each other. There are factions bent upon controlling the world's resources, by promulgating rules rigged in their favor to preserve their influence. All this is by the brute force of military power that certain countries have mustered to gather.

The pivotal question is, "Who owns the world and its resources?" The secondary question is, "Who is ultimately responsible for keeping humanity safe?"

My answer to the first question is, citizens of the world; the second, no one currently. Let me explain.

The world has now shrunk to arm's reach. But more so, it is tightly integrated. For one thing, world trade has brought us together as never before, not for any ideological, humanitarian, or philanthropic reasons, but for pure economics. However, world trade has not positively influenced other aspects that matter even more. For one thing, trade has not given the overarching motivation to live amicably with other countries. Countries simply do not trust each other in most cases.

The world is divided quite sharply, over ideologies, and much because many large powers are not totally democratic. The USA, conceived as democratic, is rather a republic. The president is not chosen by direct vote, but by electoral votes (also, for example, 23 states with a cumulative population of 40 million elect 46 senators, while one state, California, with the same 40 million people will elect only two senators). Meanwhile, the two parties are sharply divided as to how to govern the country. The other two superpowers, China and Russia, are authoritarian. Many other countries are similarly semi- or non-democratic or autocratic, where citizens do not have much say in the governance of the country.

The fact is that, at any moment in time, the world is governed by a scant few hundred individuals who have quite a bit of decision-making power that impacts about 7 billion people. Many of these individuals are quite happy to have and benefit from this level of control. Autocrats and kings will grab power and keep their dynasties at all costs. In the more democratic countries, the top echelon will resort to control by all the artifices they have, including misrepresentation, lies, and deception. Only a small fraction of democracies will play fair and be willing to give up control fairly.

The problem is that the masses are prone to manipulation relatively easily. It could be by the dissemination of misinformation or lies, thereby exploiting people's vulnerability. With in-depth information about individuals available for sale, as collected by mega-corporations, manipulation using big data is now a sophisticated art form. Individual buying habits and social media posts now provide an accurate picture of the vulnerability of everyone. Targeted individuals are readily exploited to change opinions and get votes. This is tantamount to democracy being hijacked, aided by mega-corporations and exploited by interested parties.

Even in the USA, the most powerful country in the world for about a century, money plays a major part in winning elections. In 2017, thirty-nine percent of children in the US lived in poor households, nevertheless [67]. This richest country has sharp income inequality, with 20 percent of the population earning 50 percent of total wages [68].

The income divide then goes downhill in most of the other countries of the world, save some of the low population European countries.

The decisions related to the environment, nuclear threats, income inequality, and now the handling of a pandemic is hijacked by a few hundred people, aided by several hundred mega-corporations. The result is that most of the world's population is under siege. This may be a dark prognosis, but the data simply points in that direction.

The solution, as I see it, is to educate the population of the world so they can think clearly. They are the ones who own the world. They are the ones who should influence the direction, away from impending disaster, and toward a more prosperous, equitable, and dignified world.

As I said above, the world is now a tightly integrated place, where everyone is a stakeholder in events taking place in other parts of the world. Any disaster in one place affects everyone in all places of the world. We see this clearly in the ongoing COVID-19 debacle. One infected person in China has brought the whole world to its knees. How is it that the world population has little say in how to handle a disaster in China, Europe, or North Korea? We are all stakeholders in all major crises anywhere in the world.

We, the citizens of the world, are responsible for repairing damage to the world—the result of a badly broken system dominated by a small fraction of people. Taking this responsibility is the only way to save ourselves.

## The World Divided

As I have pointed out earlier, 71 percent of the world population live on $10 per day or less. That is about 6 billion people in the world. More than half the world's population, about 3.75 billion people, makes $5.50 per day or less. Nearly 1.8 billion people live in extreme poverty (earning less than $3.2 per day)—about half of the developing world.

These are stark realities. If you are part of the other 50 percent, making just $5.50 per day or less, what kind of life are you having? What can you afford? You will perhaps have a basic living, with food, clothing, and shelter. You would have little in your budget to afford healthcare. You will also have several children, as families in poor countries tend to have higher population growth rates. You will also die at an earlier age, as much as 13 years earlier compared to the other half of the world.

People in the top 20 percent are living in a world of their own and share extraordinarily little with the overwhelming majority. They might as well be living on a different planet, as they most likely do not even know real people, or living conditions on the other side. They would have formal education, marketable skills, and more awareness of world events. They also have disposable income to take a vacation, eat well, maintain a healthy lifestyle, and have access to medical facilities. The remainder of 80 percent has none of those items.

This chasm between the haves and have-nots is self-perpetuating. The rich get richer, as they have more influence to affect policies that impact the growth of their wealth. They also have the knowledge to invest and grow richer. The poor tend to remain poor, or may even get poorer, as they have no influence to impact the policies that will get them out of poverty. In most cases, the rich become richer by using the resources and labor of the poor, but without making any sincere effort to better their livelihood. The rich, with the benefits of wealth-building opportunities afforded by establishing corporations, can shield and isolate themselves from the masses. The wages and benefits to the poor are suppressed to benefit the profitability of rich shareholders.

The 20 percent will not be rich if the other 80 percent do not exist.

The unhygienic and debilitating living conditions of the poor have been neglected and allowed to persist. World bodies such as United Nations agencies have bragged about the dramatic lowering of extreme poverty in the last 50 years, as a matter of great satisfaction. But these are people who were below $1.25 of daily income and now they are at $1.90. So, a portion of those who were living in humiliating conditions are slightly better off, but what can they do if they break the barrier of $1.90 per day? I contend that they still have subsistence and humiliating living, and that is not much to brag about.

It does not need to be this way if opportunities are provided to all on a level playing field. I have no problems with hard-working, risk-taking entrepreneurs and innovators being rewarded, but we owe others a fair shot. We should not be allowed to rig the game by building obstacles and barriers for the benefit of the few. Policies to remove loopholes for the wealthy, give the ability to get an education for the poor, and provide healthcare to all are essential to build a just society where everyone will prosper.

The long-term impact of a divided world is substantial, and to our detriment. By all accounts, half of the world's population just getting by with $5.50 per day will grow faster. The haves is essentially too busy to seriously think about the long-term well-being of the have-nots, even when it is not in their interest to ignore the poor. Eventually, rich nations will be surrounded by an overwhelming population of poor countries who will not have enough resources to buy the products of the rich. The rich will then be left trading with the rich, sidelining the poor, and making them irrelevant.

When that happens, then the rich people or rich countries pretty much will have to live in gated communities. They will need to build walls around them, either physical or otherwise. The rich countries will be living within heavily armed borders.

As I have pointed out, the world glitters for the rich. But the problem is that the skewed control, piloted by the multinational and large businesses, and runaway consumption by the population is pushing the welfare of this world to the brink. We must look at the long-term view of where we are heading. Huge consumption, which is the basis of accumulated wealth, is non-sustainable. The amount of energy and resources required to produce consumables are increasing exponentially, even though the rate of growth for the world population will flatten or stabilized at 11 billion-plus by 2100.

## Two Classes: Decision-Makers vs. Followers

The world always had two classes. The upper class who make decisions, and the rest who are the followers. This system is from time immemorial and exists to this date. But this is not working for the current state of the world. In this state, information permeates everything then the consumers of the information are free to make up their minds, but not necessarily choosing actionable decisions. But the fact that making up the mind is possible based on the information consumed is a game-changer.

There are two ways the upper class is holding on to the power of decision-making. One is by brute force, by unilaterally making and guarding decrees and implementing them via police or military force. The other is by spreading misinformation systematically to control the minds of the governed so they will bestow power seemingly willfully. Let us look at a summary of how governments evolved from early recorded history.

The history of governments in various regions of the world can be traced from documented historical records, which are about 5000 years old [69].

Sumerians (who lived where Iraq is now located) were one of the first to establish a government about 4000 years before the birth of Christ (BCE). Writing was invented at that time. This region of southern Mesopotamia was governed by a religious leader or a King, who mandated all the poor people to work unpaid [70].

In the Indus Valley, the Harappan civilization lived in what is now Sindh, Pakistan, circa 3000 BCE. Although there is little about them in recorded history, the standardized architecture and layout of the cities and artifacts indicate that centralized governance existed [71].

Ancient Egypt, from 3000 BCE until the year 641, had an established hierarchy, with a well-documented history. In the lowest level were farmers and laborers, then artisans, scribes, district governors, royal overseers, viziers, and high priests, kings, and pharaohs (who had the absolute authority) [72].

In China, the history of the Xia dynasty, from 2070 BCE to 1600 BCE, is not well recorded. The Qin Dynasty with Emperor Qin Shi was the first Imperial dynasty. The Republic of China was established in 1912, and the Communist Party won the civil war a few decades later and formed the People's Republic of China [73].

Greece invented democracy, which is being used in many countries today, between 500 and 323 BCE. Before that, Greece had city-states run by aristocratic oligarchies (power held by special elite families) as tyrants. Intense political movements gave rise to democracy, and each city-state started practicing democracy [74].

Ancient Rome, from 753 to 1453 BCE, made great strides towards politics, codes of law, and modern government. Belonging to the social class was the predominant method of establishing voting rights, thus the common people were not participants in the government, in the former Roman Republic, which ended in 27 BCE. The Roman Empire was then established, conquering Europe, Africa, and Asia. The Roman Empire fell by 476. Italy saw many fascist regimes and wars before it became a modern republic [75].

Japan has had an established monarchy since 660 BCE, and it is still a constitutional monarchy today. From 1185 to 1868, hereditary commanders-in-chief ruled feudal Japan. Emperor Meiji Tenno established the first parliamentary system in Asia in 1889 [73].

Ancient governments had power concentrated at the very top, mostly to the king or head of state. In modern times, most countries have a constitutional republic or democratic republic, where people elect a representative government and head of state (either directly or through representatives).

I will consider a few that defy the criteria one way or another and are not democratic, such as North Korea, Syria, the Democratic Republic of the Congo, Central African Republic, Chad, Turkmenistan, Equatorial Guinea, Saudi Arabia, Tajikistan, Yemen, Guinea Bissau, Uzbekistan, Sudan, Libya, Burundi, Eritrea, Laos, Iran, Azerbaijan, Bahrain, United Arab Emirates, Djibouti, Kazakhstan, and Russia.

However, some are more democratic than others. For example, I would consider these countries to have high democratic institutions: Norway, Iceland, Sweden, New Zealand, Denmark, Ireland, Canada, United States, Finland, Australia, Switzerland, Netherlands, Luxembourg, Germany, United Kingdom, Uruguay, Austria, Mauritius, Malta, Spain, Costa Rica, South Korea, Japan, Estonia, Chile, Cape Verde, Portugal, Botswana, France, and India. About 40 percent of the world's population, or 2.8 billion people, live under a constitutional or democratic republic. The other 60 percent or more than 4.2 billion are not fully democratic.

The current state of the world population has quite a dichotomy, with a smaller proportion enjoying freedom, while most of the others are not exactly free.

## Education, Living Standards, and Health

Education has a double effect; a long culture of education creates an inclination for democracy, while the more educated a nation is, the higher likelihood of democracy. A nation that is unable to achieve primary education is doomed in its struggle to achieve a high level of democracy. My major emphasis in the last six years has been to develop the primary education school system in Bangladesh. I have seen the impact it has on the slum communities where these schools exist. Children must be brought to school at the preschool level, by age five, and are provided the basic skills and motivation that will live with them throughout their education. An emphasis on higher education must be cultivated in their formative years.

It is not by accident that a better democracy provides higher standards of living. The reasons could be various, but most importantly, as said above, democracy encourages higher education, which creates a skilled workforce and overall innovation—they are the basic building blocks of higher GDP.

Lastly, in general, better economies have better healthcare for the masses, in comparison to the nations with poor economies.

Thus, in my mind, there is a direct relationship involving democracy:

Education >> democracy >> better economy >> better healthcare.

This cause and effect are generic and there are exceptions. However, democracy must be earned, as the elite and higher classes do not relinquish power on a silver platter to the masses. It goes back to education; educated citizens value freedom and are willing to make sacrifices for it.

## A Drive for the Global Good

The world at this time is quite different from the history of government I have shared earlier. Among various threats to human existence, there are silver linings that can change it all for the better—the ubiquitous availability of technology to communicate. News travels fast from one end of the globe to another. Humans are quite connected and share in the grief that grips any part of the world, even when most are powerless to play an active role to intervene. There is a subtle unity among all—citizens of all nations—though they are not explicitly expressed.

An underlying thread of goodness among the citizens of the world remains untapped. As I said before, about 60 percent of the world population remains under siege, with nowhere to go but to live in fear. I believe the world can be united in the pursuit of the greater good by directly reaching them using technology that exists or other forms that will appear in the future.

## Democracy Outside the Western World

Let us look at what happened in 17$^{th}$ and 18$^{th}$ century Europe when a debate ensued about which forms of democracy should run the country. This was after the English civil war of 1649—over who would rule (Parliament or King Charles I)—that ended with the beheading of the king [76]. Thomas Hobbes promoted the idea that all human beings are naturally created equal and should be free to undertake whatever is desirable to survive. But enforcement was the problem, as nature does not provide any means for such a belief. So, humans should choose someone to enforce laws, Hobbes proposed. That person, Hobbes suggested, should be the king, and the king should have absolute power.

However, Hobbes' concept of absolute power to the king did not get much traction, as the drive to European Enlightenment was emerging with the concept of natural rights that preserve life, liberty, and property along with it [77].

John Locke, a professor at Oxford University, published *Two Treatises of Government* in 1689. He argued that natural rights should never be taken away, and that these are inalienable rights. This reduces the power of the sovereign (a king or a state). The king or the state must protect the inalienable rights of individuals. Thomas Jefferson echoed Locke's theory in writing the United States' Declaration of Independence, some eight decades later. Locke suggested only businessmen or property owners should be part of the representative government as they are the most knowledgeable. Others were unfit in his opinion [78].

Charles Montesquieu, born into a noble family in France, wrote *The Spirit of the Laws,* in 1748. His concept was to balance the powers among three independent branches of the government—legislative, executive, and judicial—so none will have absolute power. On June 21, 1788, the American Constitution was ratified, borrowing Montesquieu's theory of the government [79].

What was the state of the governments in the rest of the world when European and American philosophers were discussing and forming newer models of democracy (even in the face of the brutal French Revolution of 1789)? Three Muslim empires came into being: (1) Ottoman Empire in the Middle East, the Balkans, and Northern Africa, (2) the Safavid Empire in Iran, and (3) the Mughal Empire in South Asia. They had enjoyed periods of unprecedented peace, progress, and prosperity, until their decline by the end of the 19th century [80]. Nader Shah created the huge Durrani Empire in Central Asia.

In the late 18th century, Napoleon Bonaparte allied with Tipu Sultan and his father Hyder Ali in the final Anglo Mysore's war, using the unique invention of Mysorean rockets, against British East India; after four consecutive wars, however, the British prevailed [81]. The Chinese, Mongolians, and Russians fought over the Eurasian continent. By 1760, only Chinese and Russian survived. Russia was ruled by Peter the Great and then by Catherine the Great. In China, the Ming Dynasty ruled, followed by the Qing Dynasty (at which time the British saturated China with opium that started an addiction crisis) [82].

I believe no serious democratic institution was being considered in the rest of the world during the time when modern democracy was evolving in the West.

## The Spread of Democracy Guided by the American Experiment

The American Experiment was somewhat flimsy in the beginning, in the era when the first President of the United States, George Washington, saw his share of political squabbles. But one thing Washington did, which was quite unprecedented, was his voluntary resignation after two four-year terms. At the time, the two-term limit was not established in the US Constitution. This went against all the norms in human history; power would be retained by the kings until, in most cases, they died or were killed. I would say that this single act by Washington gave birth to the kind of democracy that would be a beacon of hope for the rest of the world. He had the option to kill the nascent democracy right there by clinging to the presidency as long as he could, like many other despots throughout history.

Not that it was perfect from the get-go. American slaves, native Americans, and women were excluded from equality. Many Founding Fathers had slaves, such as Thomas Jefferson (who had 600+ slaves), and George Washington (who had 200), both rich Virginia plantation owners [83]. Despite their frailties, they guided the nation in their wisdom—Jefferson, the great intellect, and Washington, the great general, who freed the nation from the British.

What happened on July 4, 1776, in Philadelphia, had repercussions throughout the world for centuries. The French Revolution—mentioned before—took place on July 14, 1789. Benito Mussolini lay dead on Piazzale Loreto in Milan on April

19, 1945. In defiance of the Russian troops, tens of thousands of protestors stormed the Hungarian Parliament Building in Budapest, on October 23, 1956. A mass rally of black students took place in Soweto, on June 16, 1976, in their desperate yearning for freedom from the Apartheid South African regime. A mass rally of students in Tiananmen Square took place on April 17, 1989, against the despotic and oppressive regime. Ukrainians had a mass protest in Euromaidan in Kyiv, on February 18, 2014, despite Russian intervention.

The U.S. played somewhat of a balanced role in the independence struggle of the Asian colonies from their European masters after the end of World War Two and granted independence to the Philippines in 1946. The ensuing Cold War with Russia saw many third world countries become independent, with varying degrees of democracy, and many under outright autocratic or military rule. The emancipation of sub-Saharan African countries from the English, French, and Belgians similarly also took place mostly in the 1950s and 1960s.

The United Nations had only 35 members in 1947, but in two decades, there were 127 members. Now there are 193 members. Although I do not think all these new countries got emancipated under the direct influence of the American Experiment, there was somewhat of a trend, and some luck, triggered by the ending of World War II.

## The Barbarism of Man

It is no secret that men are capable of immense barbarism when they are allowed or compelled to do so. Some of the most gruesome events in human history are as follows:

**An Lushan Rebellion**: Yan Dynasty was created by An Lushan who rebelled against the then-Tang Dynasty in China that lasted for 289 years (618 - 907). The rebellion lasted for eight years (755-763), with the brutal killing of 36 million people.

**Genghis Khan:** The single guy who will live in infamy for killing the most people in his lifetime—about 40 million. After conquering China, this Mongol killing machine landed in the Persian City of Nishapur, population 1.7 million, where he ordered the deaths of all inhabitants by beheading, in April 1221, and piled up all the heads like a mountain.

**Taiping Rebellion**: This killed 40 million people about the same time as the American Civil war (which killed 620,000 from 1861-65). The Qing Dynasty ruled China in 1850 and faced many problems, including the opium addiction brought by the English. A rebel named Hong Xiuquan started a religious rebellion—claiming to be the brother of Jesus Christ—that lasted 14 years, one of the bloodiest in human history. Eventually, the rebellion resulted in the death of Hong.

**The Slave Trade Across Atlantic**: Americans and Europeans kidnapped people in West Africa and shipped them as slaves to work on the plantations. They were treated brutally during transportation and in the plantations. In the ships alone, 40 percent died in 35 days of a transit journey, each ship carrying 250 to 600 slaves. About 12 million Africans were shipped over a period of 400 years, between the 15th and 19th centuries. After the civil war, the US Constitution did grant a slave the legal status of three-fifths of a person, granting freedom. About 15 million Africans perished during the history of slavery.

**World War I**: Europeans decided that rather small wars they have fought over the years with each other were not sufficient. They made two factions and engaged in a war in 1914, engulfing the whole world, while killing some 65 million people, in about four years.

**World War II**: Humans did not learn the lessons from World War One, engaged in another big war, and collectively killed about 72 million people in the conflict that started in 1939. The world was divided into two camps, called Allies and the Axis. They used the deadly weapon of the time that killed people efficiently and effectively—a killing machine that did the deed in just about six years. The most gruesome murders were perpetrated by Nazi Germany, resulting in the barbaric killing of 6 million Jews. The U.S. dropped two atomic weapons, on Aug. 6 in Hiroshima, and Aug. 9 in Nagasaki, in 1945. This resulted in 90,000 to 146,000 deaths of Japanese civilians.

**Joseph Stalin**: He gets the blame for the demise of 49 million Soviets (1917-1953), due to a combination of civil war, famine, civil war, and forced resettlement. The power-hungry premier, who wanted to hold on to the helm he gained, was solely responsible for a substantial part of the deaths. Still, in 1948—and it may surprise you—he managed to get nominated for the Nobel Prize.

**The Great Leap Forward**: This is the name given by Chairman Mao Zedong to the period 1958-1961, when 43 million people died (about 20 million died of starvation), in communist China, in an attempt to rapidly industrialize the agrarian country. However, China did become industrial, several decades later, but at a great cost.

It is not that this dark side of humans will remain in the history. Men are well equipped to organize and engender others in the most brutal ways. We always see it quite frequently and they can carry on pretty much with impunity. We must build strong protective measures to save us from our own kind. If the leaders or strongmen do not deliver cruelty to their own citizens, then their neighbors or some other country can, as international laws are weak and take a back seat to the interest of powerful countries. Politics and self-interest of strongmen has always been a threat to human values. At the same time, safeguards for the life, justice, and human rights to the poor has never been a priority.

## Decision-making: One vs. Many

It is quite established that assessment by a group is much more accurate than by one person. The average count of coins in a jar by a larger group is always more accurate than the guess by an individual. Similar is the case of decision-making. A diverse group of individuals would be able to succeed in decision-making than one individual. In the Bayesian approach to statistical analysis, the more information you feed, the more accuracy you get.

This flies flat to the idea of a gifted leader who makes decisions alone. There are high chances of a flawed decision if a leader makes it alone, using their gut feeling, or based on individual experience. However, for the decision to be more accurate, the group should have a diverse set of members, all with different sets of experiences and skills.

Diversity includes cultural diversity, such as people with different languages, nationalities, and ideology; most importantly, you need people with different points of view.

A group of homogeneous people with the same cultural backgrounds, ideologies, and points of view do not cut it. But diversity helps avoid blind spots and flawed thinking that a single individual, or homogeneous group of like-minded people can fall victim to. The culture of group decision-making should be such that the individuals are not fearful of advocating a radical or different point of view.

When you look around, you can see that a group of homogeneous people, even when large in numbers, will historically not show dramatic innovations, progress, or excellence. The herd approaches of group-thinking breed mediocrity. The biggest hindrance of culture to break free from the shackles of ignorance, flawed mental models, and inaccurate actions is their strong insistence on perpetuating their ineffective past. No bold steps, radical innovations, or difference of opinions are tolerated in the culture that deviates from their populous, but sub-par performance.

When you want a high-performance group, I would suggest the metaphor of getting marbles of different colors, sizes, shapes, and compositions. Put them in a jar and shake it up. Then lay it on the table. That is your most effective group for hedging against blind spots, avoiding flawed decision-making, while embarking on innovation and excellence.

Heterogeneity, not homogeneity, is the hallmark of progress and accurate thinking.

Most current political systems are pivoted to single decision-makers, including most democracies. The kingdoms, monarchies, oligarchies, and theocracies will most likely disallow the diversity of decision-making. I would argue that this is one reason for widespread poverty, infighting, misallocation of resources to military endeavors, wars, environmental damage, cultural and ideological fights, and the downhill spiraling of mankind.

## Loyalty to the Land

Earth was formed about 4.5 billion years ago (the age of the universe is about 14 billion years), by accretion of dust grains that were orbiting the Sun. Water came from icy asteroids from the solar system's Asteroid Belt. Photosynthetic organisms appeared after three billion years; cyanobacteria (responsible for oxygen on Earth), after 2.7 billion years; oxygen in the atmosphere, after 2.3 billion years. First land plants started half of a billion years ago; first four-legged animals, 400 million years ago; first dinosaurs appeared, 230 million years ago; dinosaurs went extinct 65 million years ago; first modern humans appeared 200,000 years ago and started language, 50,000 years ago. The recorded history of human beings is only about 6,500 years old.

Earth was one giant landmass 200 million years ago; then, the continental plates started moving quite a bit. The continents broke apart, changing the Earth, and that change continues to this day.

Let us look at our place in the universe. We belong to a galaxy called the Milky Way, which has at least 100 billion stars (like our Sun) and about the same number of planets. That is just one galaxy. The observable universe has at least 200 billion galaxies. The total number of heavenly bodies is just mind-boggling, and they are moving away from each other at the speed of two million km per hour, more than 500 times the speed of a bullet. The farther away they are, the more speed they have. Then, there is this dark energy that will make the universe significantly more massive.

When we are far, far away, it is exceedingly difficult to find Earth; it is hardly a speck in the huge, huge universe. Yet, in all of recorded history, it was passionately believed that Earth was the center of the universe, and everything revolved around it. Copernicus first suggested the Earth revolved around the sun (in addition to revolving around its axis) in 1543; this concept was so out of the ordinary that interested people studied his work only in secret because they did not want to look ridiculous. Galileo confirmed Copernicus' theory about 100 years later based on observation, using the telescope he invented. The church charged him for heresy, put him under house arrest for the rest of his life, but did spare his life when he disavowed his theory.

History brings in an interesting question. Should we be loyal to the locality to which we were born, to the country (which may have changed its association several times in its history), to the continent we belong to, to the world we belong to, to the solar system we belong to, to the galaxy we belong to, or to the universe?

## Headed North or South?

How many times have you heard that COVID-19 may have stark consequences? Perhaps every day. Yet, the possibilities continue to give us chills.

The ratio of confirmed positive to death is two to three percent. This is at least ten times more than the seasonal flu in the USA. The poor and elderly population tend to suffer the most. The immediate recourse for most of the world population, even when the vaccine is now available in the Western world, is the brute force method of quarantine, masks, and physical distancing from an infected person. But we do not know who is infected, as a person can be asymptomatic and can actively spread the disease to an unsuspecting healthy person. The reach of the pandemic is global, from almost every city to the most remote areas of the Amazon rainforest.

The world was in lockdown with varying severity for several months, but the restrictions are being lifted, even under the fear of resurgent infections due to increased mingling of people. The economy is certainly the main motivator, with an unprecedented worldwide recession, as many businesses have come to a screeching halt.

More than half a billion people may see themselves in extreme poverty, earning less than $1.95 per day. A huge population is eating less. World Vision says that 30 million children are at risk of dying [84]. This is a worldwide humanitarian crisis. The pandemic has perhaps not peaked in some of the poor nations, slated to hit hard in the coming months. In its wake, it will create an economic disaster, in addition to the pandemic, in a double punch, they can hardly sustain.

For the poorest neighborhoods of the world, hunger brings more devastation than the pandemic. The brutal truth is that the disease called hunger is ruthless. When infected, it will kill everyone it touches. COVID-19 kills only 2 percent to 3 percent of those it infects. What will the starving population choose given the option?

Humanity has hit such a crossroads, envisioned by many, but witnessed by only the survivors of the previous pandemic, and other devastations. In many respects, this is our own doing by the deadly wish of growth without any checks and balances. Rich nations will perhaps not see mass malnutrition and starvation.

Poor ones surely will, and they will be left on their own with diminishing resources, because rich nations will not have excess wealth for themselves, even if they do want to give it away.

It is no secret that the world is not equitable or fair. We never made a concerted effort to do so. We never strove to make an even playing field to lift all. We have been too consumed to guard our own territories and arcane ideologies that never made much sense, using brute force with massive military buildup. Those high-tech militaries might now be useless. Alas, we could have used the resources to build human capital worldwide.

We are not going north; we are going south, for now.

## Uniting the World

This is necessary, but a Herculean task. Looking at what humans have accomplished in a short span of time, however, I am convinced nothing is impossible.

Let us first look at some historical markers since the arrival of modern humans, the homo sapiens, in Eurasia about 125,000 to 60,000 years ago, in Australia about 40,000 years ago, and in the Americas about 15,000 years ago [85].

Humans were hunter-gatherers and lived in caves up until 12,000 years ago [86]. The advent of agriculture, domestication of animals, and the use of metal tools allowed the start of civilization some 6,000 years ago [87]. The use of iron spread only about 3,000 years ago [88]. The rise of Greek city-states started 2,800 years ago [89]. Gautama Buddha was born about 2,600 years ago [90]. The Roman Empire fell about 1,500 years ago [91]. The verses of the Holy Qur'an were compiled 1,370 years ago [92]. Santa Maria arrived in America 528 years ago [93]. The United States Constitution was written 233 years ago [94].

Major scientific discoveries have occurred over the last 500 years, and were on the heels of hundreds of years of basic developments in mathematics, astronomy, and the biological sciences. Those I would like to mention are: the Copernican System (Copernicus, 1543), gravity (Isaac Newton, 1664), electricity (Faraday, 1821), evolution (Darwin, 1859), disease from bacteria (Louis Pasteur, 1860), the Periodic Table (Mendeleev, 1869), x-ray (Roentgen, 1895), the Theory of Relativity (Einstein, 1905), the Quantum Theory (Bohr, 1922), The Big Bang Theory (Lemaitre, 1927), penicillin (Fleming, 1928), atomic energy or the atomic bomb (Manhattan Project, the 1940s), and DNA (Watson and Crick, 1953).

Let's continue with a few more human ingenuities and discoveries from more recent times: heart transplants (Barnard, 1967), the moon landing (Armstrong and Aldrin, 1969), the internet (Berners-Lee, 1969), the discovery of our 3.2 million-year-old human ancestor "Lucy" in Ethiopia (Johnson, 1974), the twin Voyager probes launched (NASA, 1977), the eradication of smallpox (World Health Organization, 1980), and the human genome was decoded (Human Genome Project, 2001).

The pace of scientific discovery is quite fast. Just in 2019, the image of a black hole was produced, and an exoplanet was discovered with water vapor that mimics Earth.

The main point I want to make is that humans are quite resourceful and capable of solving problems. If they want, they can reorganize the world to promote unity and justice for all. Let us discuss more to bring this idea home.

I have been putting together the chronology of the known events of human development; and I have looked at the flip sides of humanity, both immensely brutal, and incredibly generous and self-sacrificing. Humans are naturally driven for liberty, self-determination, and to oppress others who are vulnerable. Over hundreds of thousands of years of evolution, the human mind is programmed to be fearful. Fearful about the next meal, that others will encroach on their territory, and rob them of their land or possessions. It is buried deep in our brains' wiring—humans are incredibly untrustworthy, unfair, and self-centered. This is the reason why layer after layer of laws have been created, the police force established, and incarceration facilities put in place throughout human history. All these aims just to protect one man from another.

Unfortunately, this inflection point, the point where the human brain transcends self-preservation as the main impulse for selflessness, requires a rewiring of the brain. I believe the best way to rewire is from childhood. Opportunity is lost when the child grows up and mingles with the world, deeply ingrained in a flawed mental model. The world simply reinforces what we already have rather than countering that to live against our natural impulses.

We need to capitalize on our other instincts to be generous and considerate, not self-centered. That is one reason I have concentrated on preschool education, for children living in slums. If we care for children when they need it the most, the children will have a mental model of generosity and kindness toward others. That is when we have the best chance of rewiring the brain.

It is of interest that 39 percent of the world population have no formal education at all; that is some 2.7 billion people. Further, only 6.7 percent of the world population has a college degree, and that is about half a billion people. The other 3.8 billion has some formal education, but not a college degree [95]. A college degree does change the brain structure and provides a basis for increased cognitive abilities. An interesting feature of the brain is that each time we learn something and practice it, the number of synapses between neurons increases, changing the structure of the brain. The more we learn, the more the brain structure improves, so we can better retrieve information or innovate. Further, higher education has many other benefits, including better health, more political awareness, and more accepting of other points of view.

We can certainly improve human capital dramatically by educating the 2.7 billion people with no formal education, and an additional 3.8 billion who do not have a college degree. That is a whopping 6.5 billion people, or 93 percent of the world population. This is something that appears to be impossible, except when you look at the resources spent on militarizing the world.

In 2018, total military spending was $3.4 trillion USD ($1.67 trillion in the US, and $1.73 trillion for the rest of the world). That adds up to about $500 USD for each man, woman, and child in the world. This military budget, if repurposed, can make a big dent in educating the world. Now, what is the return on investment of this significant military spending? I would say none, and if someone insists on it, I can at least say that the return is hardly worthwhile. Is the investment buying security, better market share, greater prestige, or getting bigger worldwide resources? My answer would be no. It is counterproductive, as it increases fear, insecurity, mistrust while promoting war.

If you invest the same in education, the world will be a different place, with people having better health, wealth, and happiness. The diverse populations in the world will have something in common—the use of education to better understand each other with open minds. Trust among people will increase, and nations will not require huge military spending.

The world can achieve the feat of educating all its inhabitants. This should be the third world war—the war against no formal education for 2.7 billion people, and increased education for 3.8 billion, so all achieve the knowledge equivalent to a college degree. This will be a step towards homogenizing the world at the same level, so they will work together, rather than being in perpetual cognitive dissonance.

Let us look at other aspects of world unity. Does the leader of a country represent the aspirations of their people? Do we need a single leader to lead a nation? Only kings and dictators rule a nation, but they pretty much do it by force, not with the consent of the people. A leader is chosen by the citizens to show the way. Citizens have trust in the leader and are willing to follow them. But how wise is it to choose a single person who will make crucial decisions?

For the sake of argument, let's ignore a few nations who can claim to have the checks and balances to monitor the leader, and stop him or her from making insane decisions that will endanger the lives of their citizens, and those outside the country. For most countries in the world, leaders have incredible power, treat the citizens as their subjects, do not care about their aspirations, or may not even bother to understand them.

The power of one person over another, however slight it may be, is subject to abuse. The more the power, the more abusive the relationship could be. Humans do not function well when bestowed with huge amounts of power—it is simply not in our nature. Yet, humans are prone to surrender to a higher authority. Life is tough, and then we die (forgive me for using this cliché), so we feel the need to hang on to anything, or anyone, who will save us.

We are, by our very nature, quite frail, subject to many wrong decisions and unethical conduct. In the meantime, a charismatic leader appears, a mythical savior, and we are more than willing to surrender. And therein lies the problem. A leader with huge power is incompatible to the well-being of the people, no matter how hard we try. And there he or she is, the head of the country, everywhere in the world.

The whole system of one-person leadership is flawed, yet the citizens of the world have continued to condone it.

The world has seen one-person leadership as an established fact from the beginning of civilization, starting from the kings and queens, then dictators, fascists, and totalitarians. In modern times, there are so-called democratically elected leaders who have dominated the political leadership for decades.

For example, Russia's Vladimir Putin was elected four times, and his term will end in 2024. It is said that Putin may serve longer than Russian dictator Joseph Stalin, who held power for more than 33 years. Others holding long office terms are Nursultan Nazarbayev of Kazakhstan since 1984; Ayatollah Ali Khamenei of Iran since 1981; Teodoro Obiang Nguema Mbasogo of Equatorial Guinea since 1979; Denis Sassou Nguesso of Republic of Congo since 1979; Paul Biya of Cameroon since 1982; Xi Jinping of China since 2013, but he can be the president for life because the term-limit has been removed; and Bashar al-Assad of Syria since 2000.

Some of the others who have held power for long periods are Hun Sen of Cambodia, 35 years; Yoweri Museveni of Uganda, 34 years; Mobutu Sese Seko of Zaire (now the Democratic Republic of Congo), 32 years; Idriss Deby of Chad, 29 years; Emomali Rahmon of Tajikistan, 27 years; Isaias Afwerki of Eritrea, 27 years; Paul Kagame of Rwanda, 25 years; Zine Al-Abidine Bin Ali of Tunisia, 23 years; Alexander Lukashenko of Belarus,

25 years (now facing strong resistance); Daniel Ortega of Nicaragua, 22 years; and Tuilaepa Aiono Sailele Malielegaoi of Samoa, 21 years.

Then there are disgraced corrupt leaders who have embezzled money from their governments. Some examples are: Mohamed Suharto, President of Indonesia, who embezzled $15 to $35 billion; Ferdinand Marcos of Philippines, $5 to $10 billion; Mobutu Sese Seko of the Congo, $4 to $5 billion; Sani Abacha of Nigeria, $2 to $5 billion; Zine El-Abidine Ben Ali of Tunisia, $1 to $2.6 billion; Slobodan Milosevic of Serbia/Yugoslavia, $1 billion; Jean-Claude Duvalier of Haiti, $300 to $800 million; Alberto Fujimori of Peru, $600 million; Pavlo Lazarenko of Ukraine, $114 to $200 million; and Arnoldo Aleman of Nicaragua, $100 million.

Why would a single person hold political office for such long periods of time? And why do powerful people succumb to corruption?

Let me first say the obvious: corruption is not limited to the heads of countries. In fact, in many developing nations, corruption is embedded in the fabric of the system of governance. In some cases, it is built into the culture, weakening the economic system, and undermining competition.

The head of state would hold on to power for only one reason. Power is intoxicating and strokes the ego as nothing else does. I have said before that, in many cases, humans are unable to function rationally when given power over others. Unless the system of checks and balances is strong, the person at the head of the state will do everything to hold their power, with only a few rare exceptions.

An already rich person will succumb to embezzlement for only one reason: greed. A rich man may not need any more money, certainly not millions and billions of dollars, because he or she will not be able to use it. There is no point accumulating that much wealth, certainly not by embezzlement. We do hear of many heads of state, or super-rich people, who go to jail for unlawful practices, including tax fraud. I cannot imagine a rich man in jail while they have enough resources to live comfortably without piling up wealth using illicit practices. Who, in a rational state of mind, would choose a life of infamy and shame, and possibly go to jail, when they can live a perfect life without that?

It is best that power is not concentrated in one person. It is much better if power is dispersed and the world is united in the pursuit of the hardest problem we are now facing, as discussed in length before: the survival of the human race on Earth as we know it.

## The Disease Called Racism

Even though Charles Darwin may not be a racist, his half-cousin, Francis Galton (1822 to 1911), certainly was. He wrote quite horrible stuff about "Negros," "Hindoos," and "Arabs." Galton coined the term "eugenics." Winston Churchill (1874 to 1965) was in favor of neutering of the "feeble-minded," along with Franklin D. Roosevelt (1882 to 1945)—both admirers of

Galton [96]. The point is that racism has been pervasive among the most learned people, and the belief has been entrenched in the human psyche over the years.

If anything, the completion of human genome sequencing in 2003, followed by hundreds of thousands of DNA testing, has taught us that there is no basis of genetic difference among those with black, white, or brown skin. And orange, green, burgundy, or any other color for that matter. There is no genetic difference between Christians, Muslims, Jews, Hindus, Zoroastrians, or Buddhists.

Genetic testing of two European descendants may reveal that they are genetically closer to an African descendant than to each other [97]. Thus, the race is in the human mind, just visual and a myth. Any person is a mix of their ancestors who were crossbred over hundreds of thousands of years.

Even when discussing a disease, we do not say that, for example, cystic fibrosis is a "black" or "white" disease—we would say that it is prevalent in Northern European or sub-Saharan African.

Race as biology is defunct. Race as a social construct is different—it is based on culture, religion, language, rich or poor, education, and a sense of tribe.

If someone is a racist because of biology, he is ignorant; if for a social construct, he is a bigot because of the way his mind has developed.

## Education Combats Racism

The history of racism in America is pervasive. The basic motivation was greed when slaves were abducted from West Africa to work in cotton fields. But, by no means, is racism limited to one or two countries; it is a world phenomenon. History is replete with racial discrimination. Combatting racism is a big topic, and proposed solutions never seem to work.

Just to simplify for the sake of brevity, people on the receiving end, on the one hand, are poor, uneducated, unhealthy, slum dwellers, working-class, and exploited. The perpetrators, on the other hand, are wealthy, educated, healthy, homeowners, elite, and exploiters. To be wealthy, you ultimately need low-cost workers. In the pursuit of wealth, morality takes a back-seat, and human rights are the casualty. The upper class needs to keep the lower class in their place to keep the flow of cheap labor.

They will make up reasons to keep the status quo. Among other things, artificially created discrimination would erect a barrier to isolate and stop the upward mobility of the lower class. Everyone would see this, and, for all practical purposes, tacitly ignore it. This happens over decades and centuries. Nothing changes. Exploiters do not really care. Extreme capitalism, centered on greed first and humanity second, is far too ingrained in us to be shaken.

Therein lies the struggle. Occasionally, the face of resistance raises the head, and elites will simply wait it out, or use all kinds of ploys to eliminate it, including force. Over time, the status quo will prevail. It always has. For example, schools here are funded substantially by the taxpayers' money, and in the wealthy neighborhoods far more money becomes available than in poorer neighborhoods. With this system, the poor will always have inferior education by design. If we could change one thing, all the struggle going on right now should immediately change that.

My work in Bangladesh, educating the children of slum dwellers over the last six years, has given me some insight, even when it is not the same construct. The education of children is my hammer, and I solve all problems with that hammer. I am quite biased in favor of the higher education of children in slums. I believe it is essential if we want to make any changes.

I already see this play out in the USA, where I have been living for the last 40 years. Arriving from Pakistan, I did not have any money when I landed in the USA, like many, many other immigrants. I had my engineering degree from Pakistan, and I got an opportunity to attend Iowa State University in the Nuclear Engineering department with a teaching assistant job that paid for my living. The point is only due to education was I able to get jobs and keep my head above water. If I can do that from scratch, anyone else can too. Now, I understand there are many things that are different, including 400 years of abusive history my parents did not endure, even when my family has encountered their own trauma, and when my father was killed in a racial riot.

I started with the same model of children's education at one center city location here in the Philadelphia area that I am implementing in Bangladesh. I am having ups and downs in keeping that afloat as the challenges here are different and, in some ways, more restrictive. I find reaching the community difficult in order to emphasize the value of educating their children. If I can communicate one thing to the parents, it will be this. Nothing you are doing is important. Do one thing. Make sure that your children are educated. Use all the resources that you can muster to make that happen.

Not only that, but make sure your children are HIGHLY educated. If you can accomplish that, then the world around you will change. Racism will hide from you, and I secretly wish I can be a part of that change here in America.

I believe that pragmatic education implemented on a massive scale is the only way we can abolish racism. We can have "herd immunity" for racism—if enough people are highly educated, only a few will carry the disease and will not harm society as a whole. There is no vaccine that can be developed to combat the self-created disease called racism, unfortunately.

## The Opportunist

A question: Are human beings inherently good, inherently bad, or just opportunists who are required to be under checks and balances? I argue that we are the last one.

History is replete with instances of human beings who have accomplished incredible selfless deeds related to acts of compassion, forgiveness, sportsmanship, and humanity. On the flip side, as I have noted earlier, history is full of human acts of viciousness, cruelty, barbarism, and ruthlessness. These are the two sides of humans, but they are unpredictable. You are never 100 percent sure which side will turn up under varied circumstances.

If greed is a great motivator, and if it is also good for everyone else, then all sides win. Extreme poverty, defined by earnings of less than $1.90 per day, plummeted in half in the decades between 1990 and 2010, and a whopping billion people were lifted out of poverty [98]. That is capitalism at its finest.

The flip side is that the rich got richer. Over the last fifty years, the top 1 percent of Americans have nearly doubled their national income shares, while the poor's income has remained essentially the same. An estimated 40 percent of the U.S. population are either poor or low-income [99]. Unfortunately, this is also Karl Marx's assertion that the rich get richer by decreasing the workers' earnings, and after a certain point, the poor workers do not take it anymore. I do not think that this is quite true in the USA, as wages may not be at the tipping point yet. However, 71 percent of the population in the world earn less than $10 per day, and 50 percent earn less than $5.50 per day, as I have repeatedly said.

Capitalism converts opportunity into wealth by forcing competition and efficiency, and it has served humanity well so far. This has turned humans into opportunists, which is not bad until greed kicks into full gear. Greed has resulted in a stark inequity of wealth between rich and poor, environmental degradation, the concentration of power to the few, the erosion of human rights, and a threat to human existence. This has happened quite rapidly over the decades rather than centuries.

An interesting feature of extreme capitalism is the concentration of wealth in just a few hands. Only about eight people in the world collectively have the same amount of wealth as the lower 50 percent of the world population [8]. That is eight people equal to 3.5 billion people. This is simply bizarre and unconscionable. This is extreme capitalism in full gear.

It is not that the poor are subhuman with lower brain capacity—it is simply that the whole playing field is rigged by the system, so they remain uneducated, uninsured, unresourceful, and live paycheck to paycheck. The poor of the world are just unable to catch a break and reach their potential.

Ultimately, humans are the great opportunists for personal gains, but are unable to convert that for the greater social good. We need to devise ways of checks and balances, so the policies and the associated concentration of power do not accrue to a few people at the top. Humans need this so society remains safe from their compulsive nature of being unpredictably good or bad.

## The World in Frustration

The world has quickly caught up with the protests in the USA because of police brutality, resulting in the murder of George Floyd, an African American, in Minneapolis, Minnesota. Four hundred years of racial segregation has come to a flashpoint. The world is engaging and rallying, showing their disgust for racism.

There is something deeper in the works. The undercurrent may be more incisive—a clash with the elites who have rigged the whole system to perpetually undermine the working class. The world is clearly divided between those who are struggling, and they are the overwhelming majority—some 80 percent of the world population—who are under siege by the 20 percent.

Eighty percent of the world barely makes enough for a living. They have no means to get the education they need to compete with the highly educated elite class. They are hand to mouth, and hidden, while the world glitters for the upper echelon.

The poor remain invisible and unable to fully participate in the world we live in. They cannot eat the incredible food in great restaurants, read the great books of our times, shop for high-end products, enjoy contemporary houses with furnishings, or educate their children so their dreams are possible.

On top of all that, there is a disdain for the lower class because of associated discrimination. People are classified in many ways—the color of their skin, nationality, language spoken, religion, sexual orientation, and disability. Women of the world are subjugated in all possible ways—and according to former U.S. president Jimmy Carter, who spent quite a bit of time studying this issue, men simply don't care about it.

Big businesses are focused on the short-term return of shareholders' investments—a concept that begs for expansion to serve customers, employees, and society as a whole. It would be nice if a corporation's main motto were "do no harm"—to devote themselves to the well-being of the communities they serve and the environment.

I believe the world is outraged not only about the racism against Black Americans but also about the worldwide deprivation and injustice to all segments of society. The upper class has created a make-believe world that accumulates wealth for a few while others subsist by serving them. In the meantime, hatred and fragmentation of communities are of no consequence to them. This mindset is nothing new. Look at hundreds of years of history, and most will agree that this has been the norm all over the world.

The bottom rung is divided and conflicted all over the world, by design. Poor white people fight with poor Black people, but the context of a 400-year-old history of slavery may not be relevant among them. Slavery was the creation of a few to exploit the masses. I believe racial hatred was sowed and perpetuated by elites from the get-go to serve their needs.

A police officer in the USA earns about $21/hour [100]; the average American makes around $27/hour [101]; the bottom 20 percent make $11/hour; the top 20 percent of the Americans make about $32/hour; the top 5 percent make $58/hour [102]. The average African American makes around $12 per hour [103]. Consistently low wages of a minority, over decades, is a telltale sign of their place in society and how they are viewed and treated.

There is no reason for a large population to be subservient over a long period of time since each person comes with a brain that is no different than those of the elite class. It is the elite members of society who create the conditions of subjugation by imposing laws and policies most conducive for their retention of power.

Look at the upper rung of people in any country, including the USA. They are all rich, extremely resourceful, and out of touch with normal ways of life for the general population. Many do not go to a grocery store, nor can they tell you the price of rice. The world is frustrated because there is no justice for most of us. It is to the point that we can't breathe.

## The Man from Leh

I ended up in Leh, India, in May 2006 in the wake of my rendezvous—crisscrossing India in 2006 and 2007—and had a chance meeting with Mohammad Ali Khan. He was from a picturesque village near Skardu, Kashmir, and was working for the city as a researcher analyzing data for future projects in the Ladakh region surrounding Leh. It is said that the whole culture of a locality can be given away by a single individual. I don't know if that is true, but if that is the case, then Mohammad Ali Khan provided the window for my insight into a remarkable culture. I felt like I was on another planet, mingling with people of different times.

Leh is the capital of Ladakh, with a population of 30,000. Its altitude of 11,562 feet makes the oxygen level lower than normal. When I landed by air, I planned to do my routine run, but I quickly realized that I am experiencing dizziness due to height and remembered that I needed to acclimatize for a day.

I met Mohammad Ali Khan on the steps of the old Jama Masjid (mosque), constructed between 1666 and 1667, as I came out after Friday prayer. There he was, smiling and asking where I was from; this was a small place, and he had never seen me before. We started talking, and he invited me to a small coffee shop. He spoke well—I found his Urdu accent quite enchanting—and he was well versed in the history and current affairs of the region. He invited me to his house for dinner that night.

He picked me up from the hotel, and we walked to his residence, only about 20 minutes away. The area appeared dark, but he reached for the door of his house, which was a clean and carpeted small room. I left my shoes at the door, a custom we follow in our home as well. It was a long time ago, and I don't remember if the room was lit by an electric bulb or candles. He introduced his daughter who was going to high school. His wife and the rest of his children lived in their village residence.

His daughter came to live with him in Leh to go to school. She was a nice soft-spoken girl who was extremely interested in knowing what I was doing in Leh and how I lived in the U.S.A. She was very enthusiastic about going to college and was opposed to early marriage even though it was the custom in their family, and her father agreed wholeheartedly. I just hope she has achieved her goals.

They talked quite a bit about their hometown village near Skardu, and compared that to Switzerland, which he never visited. If he did, he would know that his place was perhaps better by the description and the pictures they showed. Technology had not infiltrated his hometown that much, and he had it pristine, surrounded by the scenic meadows, at the confluence of the Indus and Shigar Rivers, surrounded by the Karakoram and Himalayan range that has peaks such as K2, the Gasherbrum, Broad Peak, and Trango Towers. What a place to live and grow up!

What surprised me the most were the books all over that room. He and his daughter definitely liked to read. He completed his bachelor's degree in the Urdu Language at Aligarh Muslim University Board. He was from an educated family—his grandfather was a recognized poet in the Bulki language, which was his mother tongue. He wrote in the local papers, was a poet, and was writing a book, entitled *Aina-e-Baltistan* (*Mirror of Baltistan*)—a history of the Gilgit-Baltistan area. I sincerely hope he finished and published his book.

In my interview, he recited poetry that was quite poignant about the fleeting nature of our life on Earth. The richness of his life, his polite mannerism, and his hospitality was something I will always remember. I never got in touch with him again, but I hope he is well and has accomplished all he deserves.

# Extending the Work in Bangladesh

It all starts with the lack of adequate income. One major reason for poverty is the absence of emphasis on education, and the first frontier is the education of children. The grim fact is that a low-income population does not have the resources, ambition, and know-how to get into the school system. If children do get to the classroom, there is a substantial likelihood that they will drop out based on poor performance or the lure of child labor.

Our grassroots approach brings small children – ages 4.5 to five—into the classroom in the middle of the slum population and provides them with high-quality preschool education for one year. After graduation, we admit them to Grade 1 in government or private primary schools.

We then make sure that the students do not drop out. This we do by providing after-school tutoring to students in grades one through five.

Our low-cost/high-quality approach has seen phenomenal success. We have 10,000 poorest of the poor children enrolled each year.

Low-cost/high quality education >> large number of students >> higher number of graduates >> higher income.

## Educating One Child

I was talking with Dewan Wasek, our Bangladesh representative of DoPeace, when the question came up about the frustration of taking care of only a few when there are millions of children in the slums of the world. How will it change anything? DoPeace is taking care of the basic educational needs of 10,000 children yearly when it should really take care of, in all honesty, 50,000 at this time. Or perhaps, 100,000 to one million children. But, for now, we do not have the resources. So, is it worthwhile taking care of just a fraction of the deserving children?

To keep it in perspective, let us look at the implications of educating just one child. A person with a middle-class income would be able to take care of the expenses of educating one poor child if he or she is motivated enough. A middle-income person is projected to earn between $11-110 per day per person, while a poor person is the one who makes less than $1.9 per person per day. A person making between $1.9 and $11 is considered financially vulnerable. Then, half of the world's population are in this bracket (poor plus vulnerable)—that is a whopping 3.8 billion people. The silver lining is that half the world population is at the tipping point of being middle-class for the first time in its history of 10,000 years of recorded history [104]. Even then, I consider a vulnerable 3.8 billion to be unacceptably high. With our model of expenses of $12 per year to educate one child, we can make the education of each disadvantaged child of the world a possibility.

Let us say you are a person with middle-class earnings, and you want to take care of educating one child. However, the fact is that you cannot educate only one child, because the child is in the middle of a community. First, the household is affected, starting with the siblings. The parents get a new perspective when their child is getting an education. Then the child has cousins, uncles, aunts, and many others who will know about the schooling of the child. The child has an influence on several members of the community at various levels. This is not a hypothetical discussion, as I have been observing this for the last six years.

We have been watching a whole community of 300 to 500 households rally around a one-room school, situated in its midst. This small place becomes the hangout for children, parents, and many others. The impact is palpable over the years.

This one child provides the motivation to several other children to be in school. As the child grows up, he or she will be more knowledgeable and will be able to make better decisions. There is a possibility that the child will pass high school; we are the witnesses to many such success stories. Further, they can go to college and move even further onward. This will not happen as a fluke, but because of the concerted effort DoPeace has been making, with an educational system that has improved over the years for such ambitious achievement.

We all know what happens when a person graduates from college. That person assumes a whole different place in life than an uneducated person in a slum. But even if a child acquires a fifth-grade education—with some reading, writing, and math skills—that is far better than being uneducated. This is like coming out of the darkness to the light—and that is how much the quality of life will change.

This person, whether with a fifth-grade education or a college degree, will be more inclined to see through a good education for their children, and perhaps those in the community. Thus, one educated person can touch many people in his or her lifetime and bring positive results.

That is the power of educating just one child.

## Innovations in Slums

While the world is on the brink of major decisions that will make or break environmental sustainability, only the top 20 percent of the population is in fact engaged at best while the rest are spectators, making $10 per day or less, hoping that everything will work out. About half of the world's population makes $5.50 per day, and they have much bigger day-to-day problems than spending time on global environmental problems.

Meanwhile, Eighty percent of the world population endures an incredibly low standard of living, and that not only includes developing nations but a significant population within many developed economies, who have severe economic inequality among the population.

When we talk about world progress in science and arts, fast-paced technologies, restaurants with amazing chefs, new life-changing discoveries, space flights to Mars and beyond, wonderful novels, innovative business approaches, dazzling new cars, and well-crafted watches, we are simply addressing 20 percent of the world population at best. Others are simply not participating at any serious level, except in amazement and bewilderment. The bullet train of elites has passed the villages with overwhelming populations who virtually live in the past century. Slowing down the train to pick up the rest is not even seriously considered.

Eighty percent of the world population needs to be retooled and armed with education, preferably higher education. At the very least, the highest priority must be placed on educating children. Even when we undertake the education of 10 percent of the world population, that would be a quarter of a billion children living in low-income spaces in developing nations. Many children are in relatively low-income brackets in developed nations as well, which means higher education is difficult.

High income (20 percent of the world population) >> high quality of life >> relevant to world progress.

Low income (80 percent of the world population) >> low quality of life >> irrelevant to world progress.

## Motivate and Fire Up the Excellence

When I look back at my childhood days, I believe I was motivated by some of the friends I had. I captured this desire to achieve and make a difference. Even though I never did anything earthshaking, my aspirations were palpable to the point where I was disappointed by the age of 15 or 16 because I hadn't done anything extraordinary.

When I think about it now, some 55 years later, I am a little surprised by my early motivation. However, the point is that early motivation is key for anyone to pursue extraordinary dreams. I believe every child has the capability to dream big, but some are not as lucky to encounter someone who will ignite such desire.

Providing motivation in early childhood is something severely lacking worldwide, but especially with children in slums. Most of them will likely not have any mentor to motivate them for high achievement. A child's mindset is established through the prism of their parents and the community they live in. Their bar is naturally set extremely low from the get-go. Higher education is neither on their horizon nor is a zeal to achieve beyond the barriers the community unwittingly imposes.

The lack of concerted and systematic efforts to provide an impetus for high achievement is a worldwide phenomenon. Only a handful get this, and most of them from their already accomplished parents, extended family, friends, or teachers. A serious plan to reach out to the children in primary and high school, to provide motivational workshops, and one-on-one sessions is high-value and low-investment. In my estimate, this effort has the potential to increase educational success by 25 percent or more among the participants, a phenomenal return on investment.

The rationale is that students are in classrooms only a fraction of the day, while many of them are distracted and checked out. Only a few are paying attention, and one factor is their lack of motivation to learn the subject, or get higher grades to obtain an excellent grade-point average in primary or high school (and beyond). The traditional approach of teaching is such a colossal waste of resources and investment. However, the situation is reversed if the students are fired up in the pursuit of success, in which case they will pay more attention. Even when they are facing a mediocre teacher, and do not learn much in the classroom, they will invest their own time to catch up or find other resources to get through the material. In other words, motivated students will devote themselves to self-learning.

Self-learning is a significant source of knowledge, not only during schooling but for most of adult life. The knowledge gained during the school day is important, but the skills of how to learn new stuff is of much greater significance. In this fast-paced explosion of knowledge, old ideas are constantly updated or replaced, and the learning must continue to keep up with the progress of knowledge in a chosen field. Not only that, but an individual change careers several times in a lifetime, and that means new learning each time. What comes in handy is the capacity to relearn. Early motivation carries on throughout life, helping individuals to be relevant and ahead of the curve.

It requires the motivation to circumvent or dodge obsolescence, keep up with the moving job market, and pursue skills and new technology to be gainfully employed.

We have decided that we are going to make a concerted effort to fire up innate capabilities early at our DoPeace Learning Centers. We have developed goal setting and motivational lectures to all 60,000 children in our center of influence. Our drive is to make a difference in the lives of the poorest of the poor children by giving them the right tools so they can break from the past.

Motivate disadvantaged children >> increase desire to achieve >> reduce dropout >> more graduates >> more gainfully employed >> reduce poverty.

## Bilingual Education

One innovation we have implemented is compulsory bilingual education for our students. It is well known that a bilingual child has an advantage over a monolingual child in several ways. First, it provides for the better functioning of the brain. It brings different faculties within the brain to enhance embracing different points of view of an issue via the manifestation of language. A person speaking another language (and, additionally, who grew up in a different culture) brings another perspective, thus providing a better opportunity for better problem solving, critical thinking skills, and show signs of greater creativity and flexibility [105]

Second, each language is a window to a different world that enriches the child (or anyone) via exposure to poetry, art, and different ways of life.

Third, each language provides a new set of nuanced vocabulary for richer expression of ideas.

Fourth, English as a second language is a boon to a child in a non-English speaking country. Even when English may not be the official language in many developing nations, fluency in the language can be very beneficial for upward mobility. In many instances, English is generally used as the preferred language for research, report writing, and communication.

We are putting special emphasis on the speaking part of the English language, starting from the preschool level and all the way up to fifth grade. We are teaching 300 questions and answers at each grade, so a fifth-grade student will learn 1,500 questions and answers in different settings, paving the way for English Speaking fluency in the slums.

## Increasing the Center of Influence

As discussed above and in my previous book, our goal is to bring little children of slum dwellers into the school system and to make sure they do not drop out but continue for higher education. At the same time, and most importantly, we innovated a model that is extremely low-cost.

We have reduced the dropout rate to 5 percent or lower per year by an aggressive after-school tutoring program.

In 2020, we introduced a program to motivate students for educational excellence. We have partnered with 10 primary and secondary schools (a total of more than 3,000 students), to deliver well-structured lectures and workshops on soft skills. Each one starts with a vision, goal setting, time management, a list of tasks, priority setting, and progress measurement.

This innovation has multiple purposes. The first is our continued assistance to students who go to the DoPeace Learning Centers. Our preschool graduates are admitted to various primary schools, and only 30 of the 90 graduates from each DoPeace Learning Center come for after-school tutoring due to the limited space. The other 60 students are left to their own devices. The only thing that should keep them going is our high standard of education that covers 70 percent or more of the Grade 1 curriculum in our preschools. Thus, our children perform at the highest level at grade one. This gives them built-in motivation and skills to proceed with good standing.

However, we are now going to the same primary and high schools where our grduates are continuing. Thus, we will continue to monitor our graduates firsthand, further making sure that they continue to perform at the highest level. This ongoing assessment allows us to further strengthen our model and expand our service to motivate our students to achieve excellence.

By going to primary and secondary schools, we not only continue to serve our graduates, but also many more who never go to the DoPeace Learning Centers, thus expanding our reach and influence. And we do all this with even lower costs per student than that of operating the DoPeace Learning Centers. As a result, we are getting an even bigger bang for our buck, taking greater numbers of children in the slums under our wings.

This extension of our model has significantly increased our center of influence from 10,000 students to about 13,000 by the end of 2020, if the pandemic will subside by the end of the year. If this pilot project is successful, we will see a dramatic number of children we can influence at a substantially low cost in 2021 and beyond.

## Literacy Rate, Poverty, and GDP per Capita

It is obvious that a country's poverty will be closely correlated with a lack of education. For example, there are only 19% of the population in Niger who can read and write. Some 45% of the population lives below the national poverty line, with a gross domestic product (GDP) per capita of $544. Let us look at the data in other poor countries and see the trend of literacy rates versus wealth (or lack of wealth) in terms of GDP per capita, or the percentage of people below the poverty line. Anyone with a fifth-grade education will be literate by my definition, as he or she would have basic reading, writing, or math skills. Let's look at the data given in Table 6.

| Country | Literacy rate (%): 15 and older who can read and write | % population below the national poverty line | GDP per capita, US dollars |
|---|---|---|---|
| Niger | 19 | 45 | 460 |
| South Sudan | 27 | 66 | 302 |
| Guinea | 30 | 44 | 981 |

| | | | |
|---|---|---|---|
| Burkina Faso | 36 | 40 | 717 |
| Central African Republic | 37 | 62 | 430 |
| Chad | 38 | 40 | 681 |
| Liberia | 54 | 54 | 703 |
| Sierra Leone | 48 | 52 | 516 |
| The Gambia | 55 | 48 | 494 |
| Pakistan | 57 | 29 | 1388 |
| Mozambique | 58 | 46 | 495 |
| Guinea-Bissau | 60 | 67 | 786 |
| Haiti | 60 | 58 | 784 |
| Bangladesh | 62 | 24 | 1698 |
| Zambia | 63 | 54 | 1307 |
| Democratic Republic of Congo | 64 | 64 | 449 |
| Madagascar | 65 | 71 | 459 |
| Malawi | 66 | 51 | 351 |
| Yemen | 70 | 54 | 943 |
| Tanzania | 71 | 23 | 1104 |
| India | 71 | 22 | 2171 |

Table 6. Literacy rate by developing nations [106], [53] and Gross Domestic Product (GDP) per capita [107].

Even among poorer nations, we see a correlation between low education and poverty. If I draw a couple of graphs (see Figures 2 and 3), they look like this:

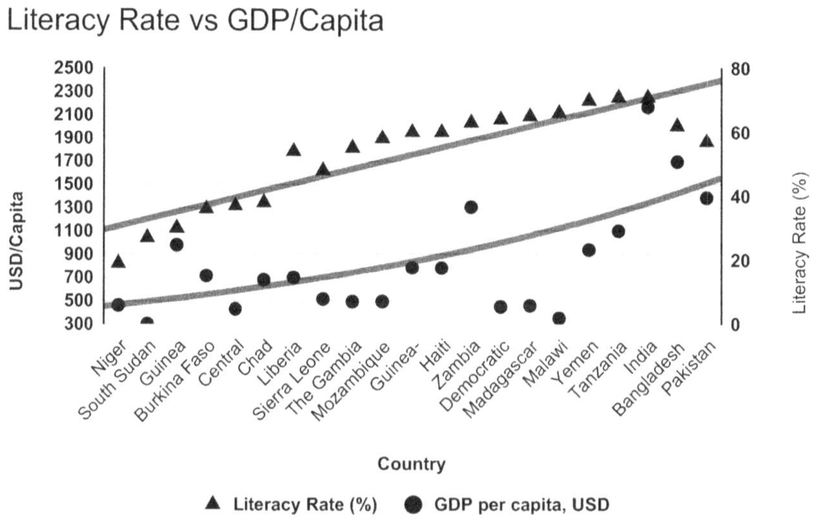


Figure 2. Some of the developing countries and the associated GDP per capita and literacy rate. The higher the literacy rate, the higher the GDP per capita.

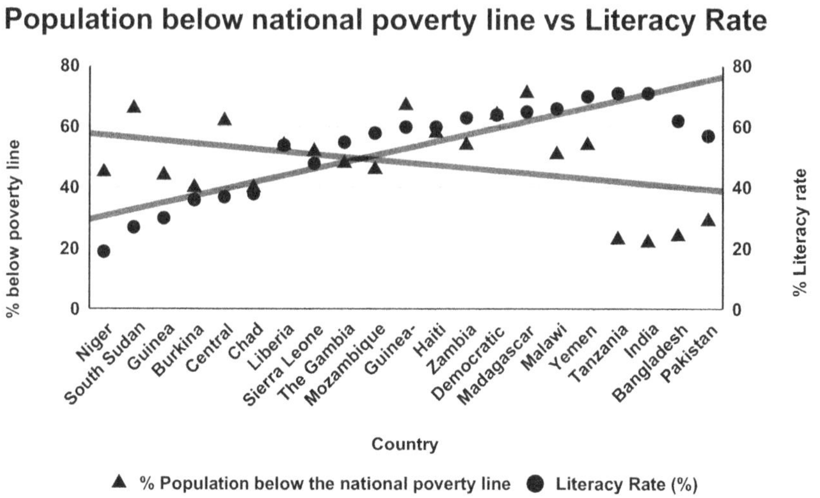


Figure 3. Some of the developing countries and the associated percentage of the population below the national poverty line, and literacy rate. The lower the literacy rate, the higher the population below the poverty line. The reverse is also true.

With the low literacy rate of Niger, the GDP per capita is below 500 USD, and 45 percent of the population is below the national poverty line. On the other hand, with the literacy rate of Bangladesh at 62 percent, the GDP per capita is below 1,698 USD, while 24 percent of the population is below the national poverty line. I am not saying that Bangladesh, India, or Pakistan, are rich countries by a long shot, but they fare better than many extremely poor African countries. There is a chance of improving the lot by educating about 50 million primary-school-age children who are out of school. And there is a proven low-cost model now available to alleviate the crisis.

## Years of Education vs. GDP

Another way to look at the relationship between education and poverty is to look at the average number of years of schooling of the entire adult population and correlate that with the country's GDP per capita. I have done that, but the data of the years of schooling is often not up to date since I could only find numbers for the year 2017 [1]. Please see the data of about 120 countries in Table 7 below.

I correlated the years of education with the GDP per capita, and you see that trend in Figure 4. The relationship is dramatic, even with this quite simple regression. Fewer than six years of average schooling of the entire adult population, the GDP is to the tune of 1,000 USD or less. But the GDP per capita shoots up as the years of education go to eight years or more.

I have kept the analysis simple and have not considered other variables such as the budget for education, political system conducive to education, and culture of education. We all know that education makes a country economically more prosperous. But what this curve indicates is that just a few additional years of education to the masses has a considerable impact on the well-being of the country.

| **Country** | **Avg. years of schooling for the adult population (2017)** | **GDP/Capita (US dollars) 2019 IMF** |
|---|---|---|
| Afghanistan | 3.8 | 544 |
| Albania | 10 | 5,373 |
| Algeria | 8 | 3,980 |
| Andorra | 10.2 | 53,000 |
| Antigua & Barbuda | 9.2 | 18,109 |
| Argentina | 9.9 | 9,887 |
| Armenia | 11.7 | 4,292 |
| Australia | 12.9 | 53,825 |
| Austria | 12.1 | 50,023 |
| Azerbaijan | 10.7 | 4,689 |
| Bahrain | 9.4 | 25,273 |
| Bangladesh | 5.8 | 1,698 |
| Belgium | 11.8 | 45,176 |
| Benin | 3.6 | 1,216 |
| Bhutan | 3.1 | 3,423 |
| Bolivia | 8.9 | 3,670 |
| Brazil | 7.8 | 8,796 |
| Burkina Faso | 1.5 | 717 |
| Burundi | 3 | 393 |

| | | |
|---|---|---|
| Cambodia | 4.8 | 1,620 |
| Cameroon | 6.3 | 1,514 |
| Canada | 13.3 | 46,213 |
| Central African Republic | 4.3 | 430 |
| Chad | 2.3 | 681 |
| Chile | 10.3 | 15,399 |
| China | 7.8 | 10,098 |
| Colombia | 8.3 | 6,508 |
| DRC | 6.8 | 500 |
| Congo, Republic of the | 6.3 | 500 |
| Cuba | 11.8 | 6,682 |
| Cyprus | 12.1 | 27,718 |
| Czech Republic | 12.7 | 23,213 |
| Denmark | 12.6 | 59,795 |
| Dominican Republic | 7.8 | 8,629 |
| Ecuador | 8.7 | 6,249 |
| Egypt | 7.2 | 3,046 |
| Ethiopia | 2.7 | 953 |
| Finland | 12.4 | 48,869 |
| France | 11.5 | 41,761 |
| Gambia, The | 3.5 | 494 |
| Georgia | 12.8 | 50,816 |
| Germany | 14.1 | 46,564 |
| Ghana | 7.1 | 2,223 |
| Greece | 10.8 | 19,974 |
| Guatemala | 6.5 | 4,616 |
| Guinea | 2.6 | 981 |
| Guinea-Bissau | 3 | 786 |
| Haiti | 5.3 | 784 |
| Honduras | 6.5 | 2,548 |
| Hong Kong | 12 | 49,334 |

| | | |
|---|---|---|
| Hungary | 11.9 | 17,463 |
| Iceland | 12.4 | 67,037 |
| India | 6.4 | 2,171 |
| Indonesia | 8 | 4,163 |
| Iran, Islamic Republic | 9.8 | 5,506 |
| Iraq | 6.8 | 5,738 |
| Ireland | 12.5 | 77,771 |
| Israel | 13 | 42,823 |
| Italy | 10.2 | 32,947 |
| Ivory Coast | Not available | 1,890 |
| Japan | 12.8 | 40,847 |
| Jordan | 10.4 | 4,386 |
| Kazakhstan | 11.8 | 9,139 |
| Kenya | 6.5 | 1,997 |
| Kuwait | 7.3 | 29,267 |
| Kyrgyzstan | 10.9 | 1,251 |
| Liberia | 4.7 | 703 |
| Libya | 7.3 | 6,923 |
| Madagascar | 6.1 | 459 |
| Malawi | 4.5 | 351 |
| Malaysia | 10.2 | 11,136 |
| Mali | 2.3 | 924 |
| Mauritania | 4.5 | 1,224 |
| Mauritius | 9.3 | 11,360 |
| Mexico | 8.6 | 10,118 |
| Morocco | 5.5 | 3,345 |
| Mozambique | 3.5 | 495 |
| Myanmar | 4.9 | 1,244 |
| Nepal | 4.9 | 1,947 |
| Netherlands | 12.2 | 52,368 |
| Niger | 2 | 460 |

| | | |
|---|---|---|
| Nigeria | 6.2 | 2366 |
| North Korea | Not available | 1,700 |
| Norway | 12.6 | 77,975 |
| Pakistan | 5.2 | 1,388 |
| Palestine | 9.1 | 3,559 |
| Peru | 9.2 | 7,046 |
| Philippines | 9.3 | 3,294 |
| Poland | 12.3 | 14,901 |
| Portugal | 9.2 | 23,013 |
| Qatar | 9.8 | 69,688 |
| Romania | 11 | 12,482 |
| Russia | 12 | 11,162 |
| Rwanda | 4.1 | 824 |
| Saudi Arabia | 9.5 | 22,865 |
| Senegal | 3 | 1,427 |
| Sierra Leone | 3.5 | 516 |
| Singapore | 11.5 | 63,987 |
| South Africa | 10.1 | 6,100 |
| South Korea | 12.1 | 31,431 |
| South Sudan | 4.8 | 302 |
| Spain | 9.8 | 29,961 |
| Sri Lanka | 10.9 | 3,946 |
| Sudan | 3.7 | 714 |
| Sweden | 12.4 | 51,242 |
| Switzerland | 13.4 | 83,717 |
| Syria | 5.1 | 790 |
| Tajikistan | 10.4 | 877 |
| Tanzania | 5.8 | 1,104 |
| Thailand | 7.6 | 7,791 |
| Togo | 4.8 | 671 |
| Trinidad & Tobago | 10.9 | 16,365 |

| | | |
|---|---|---|
| Tunisia | 7.2 | 3,287 |
| Turkey | 8 | 8,957 |
| Uganda | 6.1 | 770 |
| Ukraine | 11.3 | 3,592 |
| United Arab Emirates | 10.8 | 37,750 |
| United Kingdom | 12.9 | 41,030 |
| United States of America | 13.4 | 65,112 |
| Uruguay | 8.7 | 17,029 |
| Uzbekistan | 11.5 | 1,831 |
| Venezuela | 10.3 | 2,547 |
| Vietnam | 8.2 | 2,405 |
| Yemen | 3 | 943 |
| Zambia | 7 | 1,307 |
| Zimbabwe | 8.2 | 859 |

Table 7. Average of the total years of schooling for adult population vs. GDP per Capita in US Dollars [1].

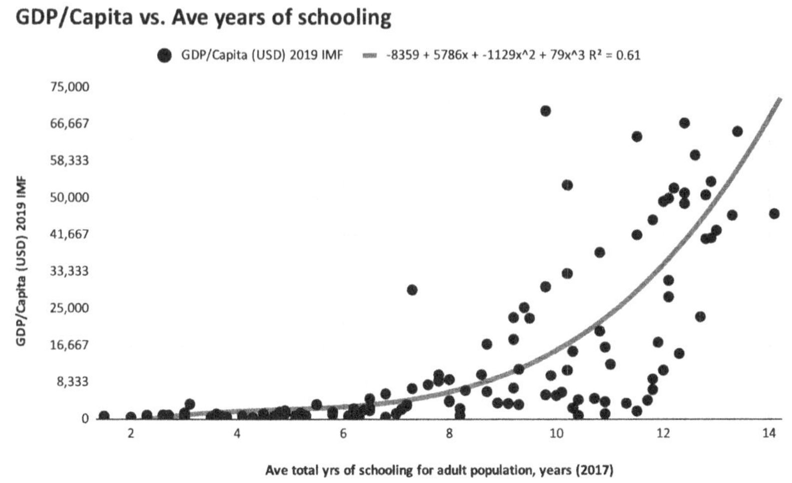


Figure 4. Average of the total years of schooling for adult population vs. GDP per capita in US Dollars from Table 2 above. The regression equation is GDP per capita $= (-8{,}359) + 5{,}786x + (-11{,}29x^2) + 79x^3$ with $R^2 = 0.61$ and x = Avg. years of schooling.

## Children Out of School and Those Below the Poverty Line

The number of primary school children out of school is an important indicator of where the prosperity of a country is heading in the future. Of all the data of impeding progress and preparing kids to emerge from poverty, children out-of-school pose as the brick wall.

Let us look at the children out of school who are primary school age. These are the children who hang around the dusty streets of urban slums or do child labor at factories or shops. Because they miss out on primary school education, they will most likely not go to school at all. There are millions of them—about 260 million globally, and 825 million (half of all young people in the world) will not have the most basic skills necessary for jobs of the future [108].

A significant number of children out of school are poor. Table 8 and the associated Figure 5 tell a story about the selected countries that have left a substantial number of children out of primary school. Those are also the poor countries, and children are not only out of school—a significant amount of them are poor. The rates for poverty and out-of-school children line up. The reverse would also be true—although I am not showing any data here. If we bring more primary-school-age children into the classroom, prosperity will not be too far behind.

In fact, DoPeace is driven by this mission, and we have brought 10,000 primary-school-age children into the classrooms every year for the last six years.

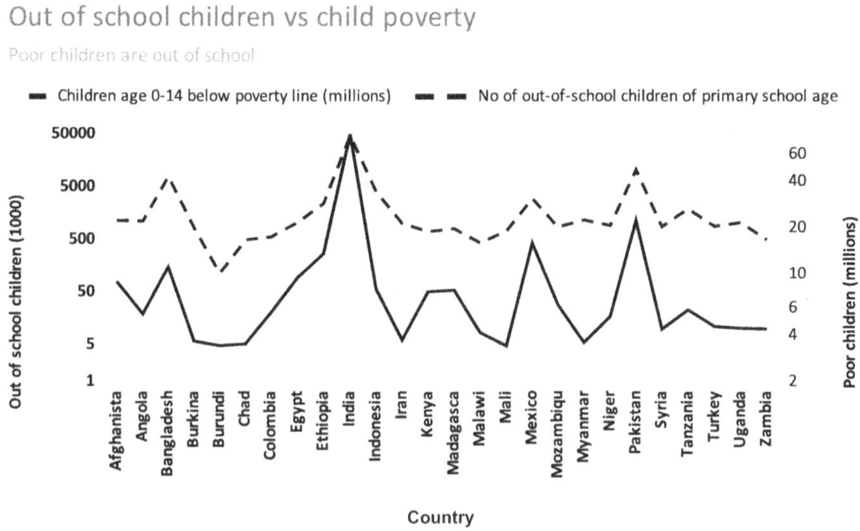


Figure 5. The number of children out of school (age 0 to 14) vs. the subset of poor children. The more children out-of-school a country has, the more children live below the poverty line. This figure is based on Table 8 below.

| Country | Children age 0 to 14 below poverty line (millions) | No. of children out of school at primary school age |
|---|---|---|
| Afghanistan | 9 | 1,148,014 |
| Angola | 5 | 1,116,691 |
| Bangladesh | 11 | 7,776,554 |
| Burkina Faso | 4 | 830,054 |
| Burundi | 3 | 114,262 |
| Chad | 4 | 494,147 |
| Colombia | 6 | 561,892 |
| Egypt | 9 | 1,057,637 |
| Ethiopia | 14 | 2,406,804 |
| India | 81 | 46,814,738 |
| Indonesia | 8 | 4,031,538 |

| | | |
|---|---|---|
| Iran | 4 | 1,011,887 |
| Kenya | 8 | 709,369 |
| Madagascar | 8 | 800,885 |
| Malawi | 4 | 432,389 |
| Mali | 3 | 727,447 |
| Mexico | 16 | 2,983,721 |
| Mozambique | 6 | 863,532 |
| Myanmar | 4 | 1,180,250 |
| Niger | 5 | 926,999 |
| Pakistan | 22 | 10,443,392 |
| Syria | 4 | 874,224 |
| Tanzania | 6 | 1,895,125 |
| Turkey | 5 | 882,827 |
| Uganda | 4 | 1,045,602 |
| Zambia | 4 | 495,692 |

Table 8. The number of children out of school (age 0 to 14) vs. the subset of poor children [109]. The more children out of school a country has, the more children live below the poverty line.

# Where Does the DoPeace Model Stand?

I have talked about a variety of critical issues the world is facing that makes our long-term survival on Earth questionable. Even the current coronavirus pandemic is our own doing, as our growth has resulted in deforestation and exposure to animal viruses. Then, the jet-set age transported the virus all over the world, causing havoc. We are optimistic that this virus will be contained soon with medicines and vaccines. But this is only a trial run for future viruses that could be more deadly.

However, the potential casualties due to current or future viruses will pale in comparison to the looming environmental catastrophe. *Waterworld*, the 1995 film depicting a post-apocalyptic world, does not appear far-fetched anymore. The window of opportunity to recover the environment is shrinking.

The nuclear threats are hanging on our heads perpetually, and the concentration of power to a few individuals in the world waits for human error (perhaps by a lunatic leader) that will trigger warheads. They have enough of them to destroy mankind many times over.

But atomic bombs are not the only weapons of mass destruction; we have chemical and biological weapons as well.

I have discussed the dangers of technology involved with genetic manipulation of species, which can be irreversibly unleashed to harm humanity. We are in the era of artificial intelligence, which can make and implement complex decisions by itself without human interference, which can be quite detrimental to the human species.

But the one that is immensely destabilizing, and hiding in plain sight, has created a crisis of epic proportions. This involves 80 percent of the world's population that is a poor underclass that struggles to make ends meet. Their rights are essentially limited by the top 20 percent; they live in all societies, communities, ideologies, castes, and creeds. No matter the political or economic system, the upper class is everywhere, which means the lower class is too.

There is one reason that the lower class is perpetual in existence, and that is because of a lack of education. The uneducated are exploited by the supposedly sharp, educated, and well-funded elites—so they become more powerful and richer—further exacerbating the chances of the lower class to rise above their circumstances.

That is where the DoPeace model comes in. The poor in the developing world is never going to get educated via traditional resources, as the funding is limited, and the classical approach of high investment in the educational infrastructure is not sustainable for them. So, the low-cost DoPeace model can be implemented to educate the poor.

Educating the lower class is the only way for them to achieve the full gamut of human rights and dignity. This needs to be done on an expedited basis.

I have discussed other chronic problems such as single-use plastics, scarcity of freshwater, unsustainable growth, unhealthy and counterproductive eating habits, excessive production, and use of energy through nonrenewable and damaging fuel. But everything pales in comparison to the suffering and misery of 80 percent of the world population.

I, therefore, propose that we embark on an aggressive program of educating the masses. This is the responsibility of each community, tribe, and nation. Politics and greed should be set aside by all, especially those in power, with an emphasis on the long-term benefit. This is best achieved by a worldwide movement by the 80 percent, whose chance of a dignified and just living is at stake, and could reach a point of no return. Nothing matters more than the drive to achieve higher formal education of the masses, perhaps in the next 10 to -20 years.

## Cost-Benefit of DoPeace Model

Over the years, I have suggested that the DoPeace model is designed for application in the slums of the world, supported by the cost-benefit analysis. It brings home the unique features it possesses and its significant impact on substantially increasing the level of education in many poor nations.

I have discussed various aspects of education and the relationship to the wealth of nations. Poor education has a direct effect on poverty. A nation that does not provide primary school education is doomed to remain in poverty until this obstacle is removed. We looked at the history of many poor nations in Africa and South Asia, and we saw the average years of education for the adult population ranging from less than two to six years or less.

The priority is misplaced. If anything, more emphasis was directed to building universities and institutions of higher education without building the base. In many cases, the whole strategy was upside down. All primary-school-age children should be in classrooms, not on the streets or working as child laborers.

I presented a silver lining earlier. This is the sweet spot that can be capitalized on. I have shown that the number of years of education in a nation (calculated as an average of the population) has a strong correlation to the national GDP per capita. Poor nations with an average education of less than six years are relegated to low GDP per capita.

But if we can increase the years of education from the low number of six up to eight years, the nation will not be so poor. I suggest that all the developing nations in Africa and South Asia can work to achieve this objective.

It is quite doable and at a relatively low cost. I have looked at the number of children out of school for countries of interest, aligned the cost of education we have in Bangladesh with the GDP per capita purchasing power parity (PPP), and came up with the monthly cost to educate all children left out. I assumed educating them for ten years and came up with a national increase in the years of schooling.

For many poor nations, the cost of education versus the benefit is substantial after adopting the DoPeace model.

There are 3.71 million children of preschool age in Afghanistan who are out of school (see Table 9 below). The average cost of education using the DoPeace model is $1 per month per child in Bangladesh and is adjusted for Afghanistan by using their GDP in terms of PPP, which is 0.46 USD. The total cost of educating 3.71 million children per month would be $1.71 million per month. In 10 years, the total increased education for preschool children will be 37.1 million years, which is an average of 1.87 years for only half the population of 38 million as an eligible base number (I considered a one-time increase of 4 percent of the population). However, I would suggest accelerating this by doubling the number of children (given the uncertainty in coming up with the total number of students out of school), and the dollars spent. This will give us 3.7 years of additional education.

Thus, in Afghanistan alone, by spending 3.4 million USD per month for ten years, the years of schooling can be increased by 3.7 years; in Bangladesh, $16 million for two years; in Burkina Faso, $1 million for one and a half years; in the Central African

Republic $0.1 million for two years; in Democratic Republic of Congo $1.6 million for 1.6 years; in Pakistan $21 million for two years; in India $133 million for 1.3 years; in Tanzania $0.56 million for one year. Please see Table 9 and the corresponding Figure 6 for countries of interest.

As you can see, this can be accomplished in only ten years, and the gains in education are substantial at an incredibly low cost.

| Country | Cost US dollars per month (million) | Increase in average schooling (years) |
|---|---|---|
| Afghanistan | 3.43 | 3.74 |
| Bangladesh | 15.55 | 1.83 |
| Burkina Faso | 0.76 | 1.57 |
| Cambodia | 1.04 | 1.31 |
| Cameroon | 1.25 | 1.21 |
| C A Republic | 0.10 | 2.01 |
| Chad | 0.33 | 1.19 |
| Congo | 1.62 | 1.58 |
| Dom Republic | 1.50 | 0.69 |
| India | 133.03 | 1.32 |
| Madagascar | 0.55 | 1.14 |
| Mexico | 24.60 | 0.90 |
| Mozambique | 0.47 | 1.09 |
| Nepal | 1.75 | 1.62 |
| Niger | 0.48 | 1.53 |
| Pakistan | 20.61 | 1.86 |
| Senegal | 0.89 | 1.47 |
| Syria | 0.32 | 1.97 |

| | | |
|---|---|---|
| Tanzania | 2.12 | 1.26 |
| Uganda | 0.96 | 0.94 |

Table 9. The monthly cost of education (derived from the experience in Bangladesh) and the calculated increase in the average formal education in years of countries of interest. Ten years of investment is assumed. Data based on GDP per capita (PPP) was used for calculations.

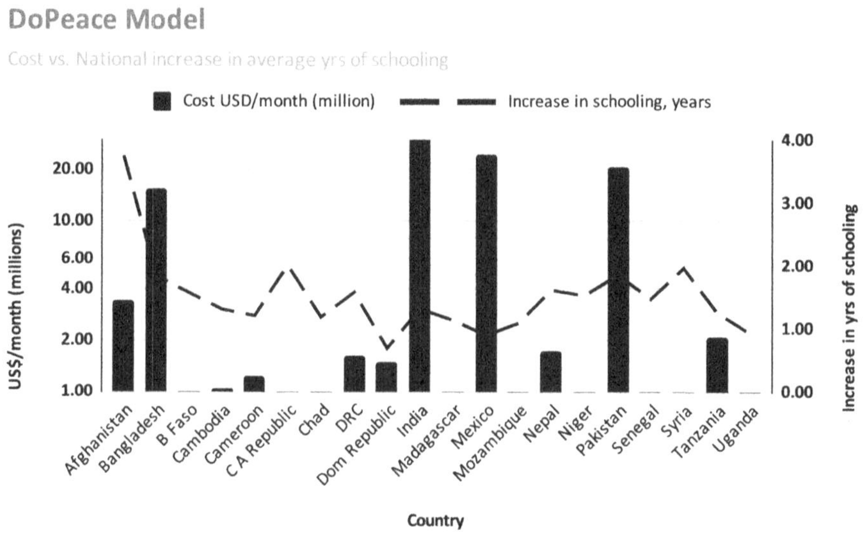


Figure 6. The monthly cost of education (derived from the experience in Bangladesh) and the calculated increase in the average formal education in years in countries of interest. Ten years of investment is assumed. GDP per capita (PPP) was used for calculations.

## Increase of GDP Using the DoPeace Model

We have taken a winding path to see quantitatively the impact of education on the well-being of a nation. We keep saying, intuitively, that education is important, but this has an ambiguous meaning. What kind of education is important for poor countries? Should they leave a substantial portion of children without primary school education and build universities and research institutions for a select few at a prohibitively high cost compared to their income? This appears to be absurd at its face value, but, in fact, that is exactly what has happened in many countries

We started by looking at the literacy rate of the countries, the percentage of the population below the national poverty line, and the GDP per capita. The results were predictable. The lower the literacy rate, the greater proportion of the population below the national poverty line, and the lower the GDP per capita. The reverse is also true. The higher the literacy rate, the greater proportion of the population above the national poverty line, and the higher the GDP per capita.

We then looked at the average years of schooling over all adults, correlated with the GDP per capita, and found a definite correlation, even when the correlation is not strong (implying that the GDP per capita is impacted by many other variables as well). However, for the sake of the first order of insight, we simply pick the lowest hanging fruit, and that is education.

The regression I found is thus:

GDP per capita (USD) = $(-8{,}359) + 5{,}786x + (-1{,}129x^2) + 79x^3$ with $R^2=0.61$, where $x$ is the average number of years of schooling for the adult population in a developing country.

It may look quite precise, but it is not, as we have ignored many of the variables I stated above. But this will serve the purpose of our discussion.

There is something startling here. There are a whole bunch of countries with an average adult education of below six years, and they are, of course, poor with low GDP per capita. But once a country's population has more than six years of education on average (seven or eight years), that country is not so poor anymore. In fact, countries with an average education of nine or ten years break away and maintain a much better standard of living.

I became curious about how many primary school-age children were out of school. I acquired the data of children aged 0 to 14 who live below the poverty line. I compared the two, and, of course, they correlate with the poor countries. I did not expect any surprises there.

I then saw an opening and introduced the DoPeace model, as this has proven to provide primary school education at a low cost in the slums of Bangladesh. At the same time, we have proven that a high quality of education can be maintained, which is the best of both worlds. Now, the cost is the major factor for poor nations, and the DoPeace model comes to the rescue to educate thousands of children, at 1 USD per child per month in Bangladesh. I then did the calculation for how much it will cost to educate children through primary school, country by country, knowing the number of children who are out of school at that age. I calibrated the cost based on our experience in Bangladesh, for many of the poor countries, using GDP (PPP), and came up with the cost per month against how much the average years of education would increase in each country in ten years.

Finally, I used the regression equation I wrote above to calculate the increase in GDP per capita due to the increased average years of education. The results are depicted in Figure 7.

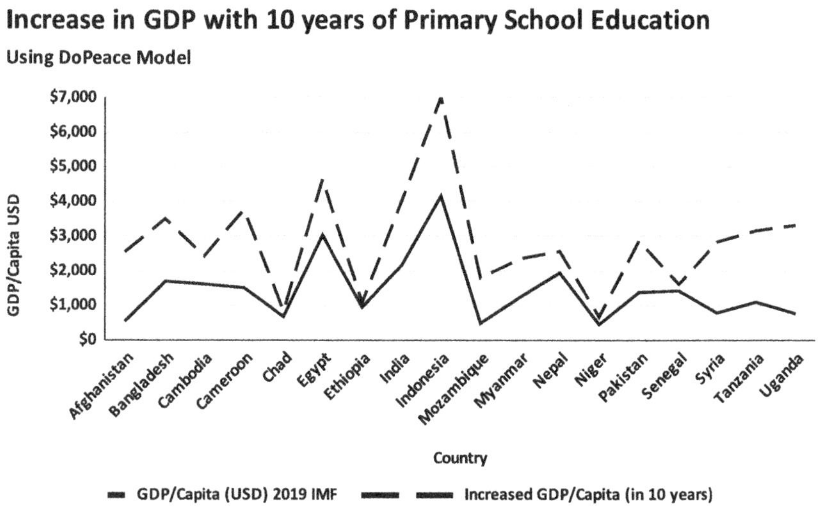


Figure 7. The increase in GDP per capita, derived from the cost of operation in Bangladesh and the regression analysis from Figure 4. GDP per capita (PPP) was used for reconciling costs in different countries, from the baseline experience in Bangladesh

We notice that with the effort to educate the children out of primary school, over a period of 10 years, there could be a considerable increase in the GDP per capita. Even though I do not think the increase would be exactly what is depicted, I do believe that that there is going to be quite an advantage to the approach I have presented.

# Connecting the Dots

I have given an overview of the current precarious status of humankind and traced the history from the beginning of time. Let us not complicate the issue. Earth is just a speck in the greater scheme of the universe. If it vanishes, no one will ever know we ever existed. Even starker than that, human beings live for a short period of time. Even when we know it very well, we do things as if our demise is far into the future. Why else do we do what we do? If I know I am going to die tomorrow, I am perhaps not going to be inclined to create mischief for others today for personal gains. But if I know that I will die tomorrow, then those personal gains mean nothing for me today, and I will have little incentive to indulge in that.

However, our strong perception is that we are not going to die tomorrow. In fact, we think our demise is far in the future. In the meantime, if I am motivated, I would like to achieve as much as I can muster. Now there is nothing wrong with achievement, as we are driven by that. The problem is that we are prone to wear blinders like a racehorse is subjected to, so he is not distracted. With blinders, we may not clearly see the real purpose of success. To achieve success, we move like a hurricane toward a goal, destroying important things in the wake of it. That is the problem.

Two of the most important aspects of our lives are giving and receiving love. A child who grows up in a loving environment is a precious human being, and he or she is the one who will shower love all over their lifetime. That is perhaps our greatest obligation—to give all the love we can to children. But this is not an obligation; this is our instinct. Not providing love goes against that instinct.

Not providing adequate love to a child is one of the greatest sources of misery to human beings. That child grows up incomplete and may never recover from the loss. In many cases, the community must bear the consequences of this loss.

The second most important thing is to provide the child with correct education, and not indoctrinating the mind with preconceived brainwashing. The purpose of education is for the child to be able to do critical thinking as he or she grows. Give a child the opportunity and ability to think and to learn, and the child will grow with this concept. It is like a tree. If you give the tree enough space and light, it will grow to its potential. Otherwise, if you put restrictions on it and confine it, it will become a bonsai tree, far less than its potential.

The third important thing is that every child must receive primary education, without exception. A country unable to provide primary education to all its children will always remain poor and will continuously be in trouble. Any attempt to achieve self-sufficiency or prosperity will remain elusive, forever.

I have shown that to be able to get out of poverty, the average education of an adult in a country should be seventh or eighth grade; to achieve prosperity, it should be ninth to 11th grade.

I have argued that for the countries of the world to achieve peace and harmony among themselves and the environment, each adult should be provided with an education equivalent to a bachelor's degree. I believe this is necessary for the survival of humanity for several reasons. First, it enhances cognitive abilities and decision-making faculties. Second, it reduces the likelihood of being exploited by the top 20 percent of elites who deliberately feed false information for their personal gain. Third, citizens of the world can be better organized to reduce the overreaching of the few hundred leaders of countries of the world who are bent upon suppressing the freedom of the masses, destroying the environment, and subjugating the bottom 80 percent to remain poor so their cheap labor can make the upper 20 percent of the population richer.

Fourth, there is a better opportunity for citizens of the world to unite and restrict the impulses of reckless top elites who destroy humanity by indulging in such pursuits as unleashing weapons of mass destruction and damaging aspects of advanced technology.

Within the last 200 years alone, men were able to bring the world to its knees by their reckless pursuits of misplaced ingenuity and selfishness. This should be a wake-up call to dramatic defensive actions through a united front. The idea that we should aggressively have a backup plan to save the human species by spreading to Mars or other planets is senseless. If we cannot make it on Earth, we are even less likely to make it on Mars. Citizens of the world must make critical decisions to save humanity right here on this planet.

The novel coronavirus teaches us that the world is intricately linked. One event in one part of the world quickly impacts all parts. Therefore, we are all stakeholders in any decision that impacts us, anywhere in the world, and we must have a say in that. We must have a say in how to protect humanity.

An extraterrestrial watching us from millions of light-years away will consider this minuscule place full of illogical and insane civilizations who are engrossed in fighting each other, yet unable to take concrete measures to stop sliding into impending demise.

The only way to avoid the unthinkable is to educate everyone and to increase the collective consciousness of civilization. This is necessary to stop the misery of inequitable distribution of resources from a few multibillionaires to the overwhelming majority of poor people who struggle daily to make ends meet.

Education to all is a required and necessary ingredient for any hope of humanity's survival. Education is a great equalizer. Let's start with primary education, which poor nations have not provided to all their children. They will have no hope of shedding this status until they can furnish this basic of human rights to children. To leave poverty, the average education of the adult population must be from seventh to eighth grade; to live reasonably well, it should be ninth to tenth grade. You start living in prosperity with an average education close to the eleventh grade or more.

But for any hope for humanity to survive, and I cannot repeat enough, the average education of citizens of the world should be equivalent to college level. Only then will the world achieve the wisdom we need to attain harmony and long-term survival.

# Epilogue

The proposals in this book may seem out of reach and out of a fantasy novel. Is it at all possible to achieve the kind of education I am suggesting to everyone on Earth? Is it possible to give even the primary school education to every child in all poor countries?

The current status of the world is nothing less than a fantasy novel if it were written 200 years ago. Who would have imagined that we would become capable of damaging Earth as we do, at the current rate? Who would have imagined that we would develop and be willing to use weapons of mass destruction that can kill humanity many times over? Who would have imagined that we will make all the technological progress to come to the brinkmanship we witness today—to the point that many are thinking that perhaps we should spread out to another planet for the survival of the human race?

If we can be so innovative as to create such conflict and mischief in such a short period of time, we can certainly be resourceful enough to elevate the mass consciousness through education. And that is the best hope I can imagine now.

# Acknowledgements

I would first like to thank my wife Naheed for all the support she has provided to continue my work with DoPeace, and her generosity with the school projects.

I must also thank Dewan Wasek, who was instrumental and a key partner in developing a successful model that has enabled us to bring thousands of children into the school system.

I would like to thank the more than 200 staff members, including teachers, supervisors, executive directors, and the School Management Committee members, who have made our enterprise possible.

My special thanks go to Zafar Khizer, AiJaz Rizvi, Manish Gorawala, Kevin Hoke, Farid Ahmed, Faizi Ahmed, Chetan Sodhi, Hira Chaudhry, and Paul Starling for their volunteer work with DoPeace.

# References


[1] M. Roser and E. Ortiz-Ospina, "Primary and Secondary Education," OurWorldInData.org, 2013. [Online]. Available: https://ourworldindata.org/grapher/projections-of-the-rate-of-no-education-based-on-current-global-education-trends-1970-2050. [Accessed November 2020].

[2] C. Vera, "OXFAM International," 9 July 2020. [Online]. Available: https://www.oxfam.org/en/research/hunger-virus-how-covid-19-fuelling-hunger-hungry-world. [Accessed November 2020].

[3] Wikipedia, "Cognative dissonance," Wikipedia, 18 November 2020. [Online]. Available: https://en.wikipedia.org/wiki/Cognitive_dissonance. [Accessed Novemnber 2020].

[4] C. Stone, D. Trisi, A. Sherman and J. Beltran, "A Guide to Statistics on Historical Trends in Income Inequality," Center on Budget and Policy Priorities, 13 January 2020. [Online]. [Accessed November 2020].

[5] National Geographic, "Nonrenewable Resources," National Geographic, 24 October 2019. [Online]. [Accessed November 2020].

[6] Union of Concerned Scientist, "Coal Power Imacts," 9 July 2019. [Online]. [Accessed November 2020].

[7] M. MacVean, "Los Angeles Times," 21 March 2014. [Online]. Available: https://www.latimes.com/health/la-xpm-2014-mar-21-la-he-keeping-stuff-20140322-story.html. [Accessed November 2020].

[8] A. Ratcliff, "OXFAM International," 16 January 2017. [Online]. Available: https://www.oxfam.org/en/press-releases/just-8-men-own-same-wealth-half-world. [Accessed November 2020].

[9] T. Worstall, "Bill Gates is not richer than 140 countries," 28 September 2013. [Online]. Available: https://www.forbes.com/sites/timworstall/2013/09/28/bill-gates-is-not-richer-than-140-nations/?sh=710e516e5ee9.

[10] H. J. Hoffman, "The Permian Extinction--When Life Nearly Came to an End," nationalgeographic.com, 6 June 2019. [Online]. Available: https://www.nationalgeographic.com/science/prehistoric-world/permian-extinction/#close. [Accessed November 2020].

[11] Wikipedia, "List of socialist states," 2 November 2020. [Online]. Available: https://en.wikipedia.org/wiki/List_of_socialist_states. [Accessed November 2020].

[12] United Nations, "World Economic Situation and Prospects 2018," United Nations, 2018. [Online]. Available: https://www.un.org/development/desa/dpad/wp-content/uploads/sites/45/publication/WESP2018_Full_Web-1.pdf. [Accessed November 2020].

[13] E. Duffin, "Poverty rates in OECD countries in 2017," statista.com, 17 January 2020. [Online]. Available: https://www.statista.com/statistics/233910/poverty-rates-in-oecd-countries/. [Accessed November 2020].

[14] The World Bank, "Nearly Half the World Lives on Less than $5.5 a Day," The World Bank, 17 October 2018. [Online]. Available: https://www.worldbank.org/en/news/press-release/2018/10/17/nearly-half-the-world-lives-on-less-than-550-a-day#:~:text=17%2C%202018%20%E2%80%94%20Economic%20advances%20around,needs%2C%20the%20World%20Bank%20said.. [Accessed November 2020].

[15] OXFAM, "Public Good or Private Wealth?," OXFAM, January 2019. [Online]. Available: https://oxfamilibrary.openrepository.com/bitstream/handle/10546/620599/bp-public-good-or-private-wealth-210119-summ-en.pdf?utm_source=indepth. [Accessed November 2020].

[16] Pew Research Center, "World Population by Income," 13 August 2015. [Online]. Available: https://www.pewresearch.org/global/interactives/global-population-by-income/. [Accessed November 2020].

[17] E. Duffin, "Percentage distribution of household income in the U.S. in 2019," statista, 5 November 2020. [Online]. Available: https://www.statista.com/statistics/203183/percentage-distribution-of-household-income-in-the-us/. [Accessed November 2020].

[18] C. Kelly, "13 sex trafficking statistics that explain the enormity of the global sex trade," USA Today, 29 July 2019. [Online]. Available: https://www.usatoday.com/story/news/investigations/2019/07/29/12-trafficking-statistics-enormity-global-sex-trade/1755192001/. [Accessed November 2020].

[19] S. Wendoh, "Female geital mutition (FGM) is a human rights violation," International Planned Parenthood Federation, 5 February 2018. [Online]. Available: https://www.ippf.org/blogs/female-genital-mutilation-fgm-human-rights-violation. [Accessed November 2020].

[20] UNESCO, "Child marriage allowed in 20 countries impending the right to education," Girld not Brides, 7 March 2018. [Online]. Available: https://www.girlsnotbrides.org/where-does-it-happen/#:~:text=Child%20marriage%20is%20a%20truly,before%20the%20age%20of%2018.. [Accessed November 2020].

[21] J. Carter, "Why I Believe the Mistreatment of Women is the Number One Human Rights Abuse," The Carter Center, 27 May 2015. [Online]. Available: https://www.cartercenter.org/news/editorials_speeches/jc-TEDWomen-may-2015.html.

[22] unicef, "Child poverty," November 2020. [Online]. Available: https://www.unicef.org/social-policy/child-poverty#:~:text=Across%20the%20world%2C%20about%20one,children%20live%20in%20extreme%20poverty. [Accessed November 2020].

[23] The Economist, "Ever more countries are banning plastic bags," The Economist, July 2019. [Online]. Available: https://www.economist.com/graphic-detail/2019/07/24/ever-more-countries-are-banning-plastic-bags. [Accessed November 2020].

[24] L. Parker, "A Whopping 91 Percent of Plastic Isn't Recycled," National Geographic, 5 July 2019. [Online]. Available: https://www.nationalgeographic.org/article/whopping-91-percent-plastic-isnt-recycled/. [Accessed November 2020].

[25] Mail Online, "Plastic is in more than 80% of TAP WATER around the world and could penetrate organs, scientists warn," Mail Online, 5 November 2020. [Online]. Available: https://www.dailymail.co.uk/health/article-4857056/Plastic-80-tap-water-world.html. [Accessed November 2020].

[26] R. Harrington, "By 2050, the oceans could have more plastic than fish," 26 January 2017. [Online]. Available: https://www.businessinsider.com/plastic-in-ocean-outweighs-fish-evidence-report-2017-1#:~:text=The%20report%20projects%20the%20oceans,and%20it's%20continuing%20to%20rise. [Accessed November 2020].

[27] International Union for Conservation of Nature, "Marine Plastics," IUCN, May 2018. [Online]. Available: https://www.iucn.org/resources/issues-briefs/marine-plastics#:~:text=strong%20and%20malleable.-,Over%20300%20million%20tons%20of%20plastic%20are%20produced%20every%20year,abundant%20items%20of%20marine%20litter.. [Accessed November 2020].

[28] T. Nace, "We're now at a million plastic bottles per minute - 91% of which are not recycled," Forbes, 26 July 2017. [Online]. Available: https://www.forbes.com/sites/trevornace/2017/07/26/million-plastic-bottles-minute-91-not-recycled/?sh=20dde376292c. [Accessed November 2020].

[29] Minnesota Pollution Control Agency, "Time for plastic diet," 26 April 2018. [Online]. Available: https://www.pca.state.mn.us/featured/time-plastic-diet#:~:text=Americans%20throw%20away%2035%20billion,%2C%20lakes%2C%20and%20the%20ocean. [Accessed November 2020].

[30] Wikipedia, "List of countries by household final consumption per capita," Wikipedia, 18 October 2020. [Online]. Available: https://en.wikipedia.org/wiki/List_of_countries_by_household_final_consumption_expenditure_per_capita. [Accessed November 2020].

[31] United Nations Development Program, "Half of world's poor are children," 20 September 2018. [Online]. Available: http://hdr.undp.org/en/content/half-worlds-poor-are-children#:~:text=Some%201.3%20billion%20people%20live,the%202018%20MPI%20is%20calculated. [Accessed November 2020].

[32] Water Footprint Calculator, "The Water footprint of Beef: Industrial vs. Pasture-Raised," GRACE Communications Foundation, 30 November 2018. [Online]. Available: https://www.watercalculator.org/footprint/water-footprint-beef-industrial-pasture/. [Accessed November 2020].

[33] Home Preservation Manual, "Learn how many trees it took to build your home?," November 2020. [Online]. Available: https://www.homepreservationmanual.com/how-many-trees-to-build-a-house/#:~:text=In%20total%2C%20building%20a%20home,for%20every%202600%20square%20feet.. [Accessed November 2020].

[34] D. Netburn, "Q&A: Carbon emissions will reach record high in 2019, thanks to the burning of fossit fuels," 3 December 2019. [Online]. Available: https://www.latimes.com/environment/story/2019-12-03/carbon-dioxide-emissions-fossil-fuels-record-high-2019#:~:text=A%20climate%20change%20milestone%20is,with%20rising%20CO2%20emissions. [Accessed November 2020].

[35] National Oceanic and Atmospheric Administration, "Ocean-Atmosphere CO2 Exchange," 23 September 2020. [Online]. Available: https://sos.noaa.gov/datasets/ocean-atmosphere-co2-exchange/#:~:text=Notable%20Features-,When%20carbon%20dioxide%20CO2%20is%20released%20into%20the%20atmosphere,certain%20areas%20of%20the%20ocean. [Accessed 2020 November].

[36] R. Lindsey, "Climate Change: Atmospheric Carbon Dioxide," Climate.gov, 14 August 2020. [Online]. Available: https://www.climate.gov/news-features/understanding-climate/climate-change-atmospheric-carbon-dioxide#:~:text=Global%20atmospheric%20carbon%20dioxide%20concentrations,for%20the%20past%20800%2C000%20years.&text=During%20these%20cycles%2C%20CO2,dashed%20lin. [Accessed November 2020].

[37] Cathy, "Green Eco Services," 14 September 2015. [Online]. Available: http://www.greenecoservices.com/how-much-water-does-it-take/.

[38] World Wildlife Fund, "The Impact of a Cotton T-Shirt," 16 January 2013. [Online]. Available: https://www.worldwildlife.org/stories/the-impact-of-a-cotton-t-shirt. [Accessed November 2020].

[39] J. Becker, "21 Surprising statistics that reveal how much stuff we actually own," Becoming Minimalist, 2015. [Online]. Available: https://www.becomingminimalist.com/clutter-stats/comment-page-3/. [Accessed November 2020].

[40] B. Jame, "We are running out of time to solve our footware problem," Concept21, 16 June 2020. [Online]. Available: https://www.concept-21.com/thoughts/footwears-sustainability-problem/. [Accessed November 2020].

[41] U.S. Department of the Interior, "How much water does it take to grow a hamberger," November 2020. [Online]. Available: https://water.usgs.gov/edu/activity-watercontent.html.

[42] M. McDermott, "From Lettuce to Beef, What's the Water Footprint of Your Food?," 11 October 2018. [Online]. Available: https://www.treehugger.com/from-lettuce-to-beef-whats-the-water-footprint-of-your-food-4858599.

[43] H. Ritchie and M. Roser, "Energy," OurWorldInData.org, 2014. [Online]. Available: https://ourworldindata.org/energy. [Accessed November 2020].

[44] E. Duffin, "Proportion of selected age groups of world population in 2020, by region," 6 October 2020. [Online]. Available: https://www.statista.com/statistics/265759/world-population-by-age-and-region/.

[45] "Population structure and aging," 16 October 2020. [Online]. Available: https://ec.europa.eu/eurostat/statistics-explained/index.php/Population_structure_and_ageing#Slightly_more_than_three_persons_of_working_age_for_every_person_aged_65_or_over.

[46] M. Roser, H. Ritchie and E. Ortiz-Ospina, "World Population Growth," OurWorldInData.org, 2013. [Online]. Available: https://ourworldindata.org/world-population-growth. [Accessed November 2020].

[47] CIA World Factbook, "The World Factbook-Population," CIA, July 2020. [Online]. Available: https://www.cia.gov/library/publications/the-world-factbook/fields/335rank.html. [Accessed November 2020].

[48] The Global Health Observatory, "Proportion of population below the international poverty line of US$1.9 per day (%)," World Health Organization, 20 August 2019. [Online]. Available: https://www.who.int/data/gho/data/indicators/indicator-details/GHO/proportion-of-population-below-the-international-poverty-line-of-us$1-90-per-day-(-). [Accessed November 2020].

[49] K. Fenz and K. Hamel, "More than half of the world's poor are children," 20 June 2019. [Online]. Available: https://www.brookings.edu/blog/future-development/2019/06/20/more-than-half-of-the-worlds-poor-are-children/. [Accessed November 2020].

[50] UNICEF, "Early childhood development: A statistical snapshot," UNICEF, 2013. [Online]. Available: https://www.unicef.org/earlychildhood/files/ECD_Brochure_FINAL_LR.pdf. [Accessed November 2020].

[51] Kyodo News, "World poverty rate to mark 1st rise in 22 yrs due to virus: U.N.," KYODO NEWS, 24 July 2020. [Online]. Available: https://english.kyodonews.net/news/2020/07/79223deb1a35-world-poverty-rate-to-mark-1st-rise-in-22-yrs-due-to-virus-un.html. [Accessed November 2020].

[52] Work4Youth, "Lack of higher education leaves millions of youth out of decent work in developing countries," United Nations-Secretary General's Envoy on Youth, 12 December 2014. [Online]. Available: https://www.un.org/youthenvoy/2014/12/lack-higher-education-leaves-millions-youth-decent-work-developing-countries/. [Accessed November 2020].

[53] The World Bank, "Poverty," 7 October 2020. [Online]. Available: https://www.worldbank.org/en/topic/poverty/overview.

[54] Council on Community Pediatrics, "Poverty and Child Health in the United States," Official Journal of the American Academy of Pediatrics, April 2016. [Online]. Available: https://pediatrics.aappublications.org/content/137/4/e20160339. [Accessed November 2020].

[55] N. LePan, "Visualizing the History of Pandemics," Visual Capitalist, 14 March 2020. [Online]. Available: https://www.visualcapitalist.com/history-of-pandemics-deadliest/. [Accessed November 2020].

[56] E. Mazareanu, "Number of scheduled passengers boarded by the global airline instry from 2004 to 2021," statista, 10 June 2020. [Online]. Available: https://www.statista.com/statistics/564717/airline-industry-passenger-traffic-globally/. [Accessed November 2020].

[57] R. Kochhar, "Seven-in-ten people globally live on $10 or less per day," Pew Research Center, 23 September 2015. [Online]. Available: https://www.pewresearch.org/fact-tank/2015/09/23/seven-in-ten-people-globally-live-on-10-or-less-per-day/. [Accessed November 2020].

[58] Johns Hopkins University of Medicine, "Coronavirus Resource Center," 8 November 2020. [Online]. Available: https://coronavirus.jhu.edu/data/mortality.

[59] H. Ritchie and M. Roser, "Causes of Death," OurWorldInData.org, December 2019. [Online]. Available: https://ourworldindata.org/causes-of-death. [Accessed November 2020].

[60] T. S. Bernard and K. Russell, "The Middle-Class Crunch: A Look at 4 Family Budgets," The New York Times, 3 October 2019. [Online]. Available: https://www.nytimes.com/interactive/2019/10/03/your-money/middle-class-income.html. [Accessed November 2020].

[61] costof.liv, "Cost of Living in Dhaka," Costof.live, 2020. [Online]. Available: https://costof.live/cost-of-living/in/dhaka. [Accessed November 2020].

[62] Trading Economics, "Bangladesh Average Monthly Income," Trading Economics, 2020. [Online]. Available: https://tradingeconomics.com/bangladesh/wages. [Accessed November 2020].

[63] E. Barone, L. Tweeten, C. Wilson and T. Law, "The Coronavirus Pandemic Has Caused Carbon Emissions To Drop. But That Likely Won't Last," Time.com, 9 July 2020. [Online]. Available: https://time.com/5864374/coronavirus-carbon-emissions/. [Accessed November 2020].

[64] The Guardian, "Coronavirus pandemic leading to huge drop in air polution," The Guardian, April 2020. [Online]. Available: https://www.theguardian.com/environment/2020/mar/23/coronavirus-pandemic-leading-to-huge-drop-in-air-pollution. [Accessed November 2020].

[65] J. McMahon, "Study: Coronavirus Lockdown Likely Saved 77,000 Lives In China Just By Reducing Pollution," Forbes.com, 16 March 2020. [Online]. Available: https://www.forbes.com/sites/jeffmcmahon/2020/03/16/coronavirus-lockdown-may-have-saved-77000-lives-in-china-just-from-pollution-reduction/?sh=7076a96b34fe. [Accessed November 2020].

[66] J. Chamie, "YaleGlobal Online," Yale University, 11 Feruary 2020. [Online]. Available: https://yaleglobal.yale.edu/content/world-population-2020-overview. [Accessed November 2020].

[67] Child Trands, "Children in Poverty," Child Trends, 28 January 2019. [Online]. Available: https://www.childtrends.org/indicators/children-in-poverty. [Accessed November 2020].

[68] Wikipedia, "Household income in the United States," September 2020. [Online]. Available: https://en.wikipedia.org/wiki/Household_income_in_the_United_States. [Accessed November 2020].

[69] Wikipedia, "Ancient history," November 2020. [Online]. Available: https://en.wikipedia.org/wiki/Ancient_history#:~:text=The%20span%20of%20recorded%20history,period%203000%20BC%20%E2%80%93%20AD%20500.. [Accessed November 2020].

[70] History.com Editors, "Sumer," History.com, 8 October 2020. [Online]. Available: https://www.history.com/topics/ancient-middle-east/sumer. [Accessed November 2020].

[71] The Editors of Encyclopaedia Britannica, "Indus civilizatgion," Encyclopædia Britannica, 03 March 2020. [Online]. Available: https://www.britannica.com/topic/Indus-civilization. [Accessed November 2020].

[72] J. J. Mark, "Social Structure in Ancient Egypt," 21 September 2017. [Online]. Available: https://www.ancient.eu/article/1123/. [Accessed November 2020].

[73] Oldest.org, "7 Oldest Governments in the World," 2020. [Online]. Available: https://www.oldest.org/politics/governments/. [Accessed November 2020].

[74] History.com Editors, "Ancient Greek Democracy," 30 September 2019. [Online]. Available: https://www.history.com/topics/ancient-greece/ancient-greece-democracy. [Accessed November 2020].

[75] History.com Editory, "Ancient Greek Democracy," 30 September 2019. [Online]. Available: https://www.history.com/topics/ancient-greece/ancient-greece-democracy. [Accessed 10 November].

[76] J. H. Ohlmeyer, "English Civil Wars," Encyclopædia Britannica, 23 October 2020. [Online]. Available: https://www.britannica.com/event/English-Civil-Wars. [Accessed November 2020].

[77] C. Friend, "Social Contract Theory," INternet Encyclopedia of Philosophy, November 2020. [Online]. Available: https://iep.utm.edu/soc-cont/. [Accessed November 2020].

[78] Constitutional Rights Foundation, "Two Visions of Government," 2016. [Online]. Available: https://www.crf-usa.org/images/t2t/pdf/HobbesorLocke.pdf. [Accessed November 2020].

[79] R. Shackleton, "Montesquieu: French political philosopher," Encyclopædia Britannica, 06 February 2020. [Online]. Available: https://www.britannica.com/biography/Montesquieu. [Accessed November 2020].

[80] S. P. Blake, "Safavid, Mughal, and Ottoman Empires," in *Time in Early Modern Islam: Calendar, Ceremony, and Chronology in the Safavid, Mughal and Ottoman Empires (pp. 21-47)*, Cambridge, Cambridge University Press, 2013, pp. 21-47.

[81] K. Szczepanski, "Biography of Tipu Sultan, the Tiger of Mysore," ThoughtCo, 25 August 2020. [Online]. Available: https://www.thoughtco.com/tipu-sultan-the-tiger-of-mysore-195494. [Accessed November 2020].

[82] P. C. Perdue, "Boundaries, Maps, and Movement: Chinese, Russian, and Mongolian empires in Early Modern Central eurasia," *The Internatinal History Review*, vol. 20, no. 2, pp. 263-286, June 1998.

[83] L. Thielen, "For the Founding Fathers, only white men deserved sights," SC Times-USA Today, 1 July 2019. [Online]. Available: https://www.sctimes.com/story/opinion/2019/07/01/founding-fathers-only-white-men-deserved-rights/1620597001/. [Accessed November 2020].

[84] World Vision, "Coronavirus: 30 million children's lives at risk from secondary effects of deadly disease," 7 April 2020. [Online]. Available: https://www.wvi.org/newsroom/world-vision-european-union/coronavirus-30-million-childrens-lives-risk-secondary-effects. [Accessed November 2020].

[85] Wikipedia, "Early human migrations," 7 November 2020. [Online]. Available: https://en.wikipedia.org/wiki/Early_human_migrations. [Accessed November 2020].

[86] S. Appleton and a. M. Willis, "Hunter-Gatherer Culture," National Geographic, 19 August 2019. [Online]. [Accessed November 2020].

[87] E. Howell, "How Long Have Humans Been On Earth?," Universe Today, 19 January 2015. [Online]. Available: https://www.universetoday.com/38125/how-long-have-humans-been-on-earth/. [Accessed November 2020].

[88] Wikipedia, "Iron Age," 12 November 2020. [Online]. Available: https://en.wikipedia.org/wiki/Iron_Age. [Accessed 22 November 2020].

[89] UShistory, "Rise of City-States: Athens and Sparta," Independence Hall Association in Philadelphia, [Online]. Available: https://www.ushistory.org/civ/5a.asp#google_vignette. [Accessed November 2020].

[90] A. Boyle, "Religious roots of Buddha's birthplace traced back 2,600 years," 25 November 2013. [Online]. Available: https://www.nbcnews.com/sciencemain/religious-roots-buddhas-birthplace-traced-back-2-600-years-2D11648772. [Accessed November 2020].

[91] S. Guess, "The end of empire," The Guardian, 19 January 2009. [Online]. Available: https://www.theguardian.com/commentisfree/cifamerica/2009/jan/19/barack-obama-rome-empire. [Accessed November 2020].

[92] Anadolu Agency, "1370 year-old Quran manuscripts unearthed in UK university," Daily Sahab, 22 July 2015. [Online]. Available: https://www.dailysabah.com/religion/2015/07/22/1370-year-old-quran-manuscripts-unearthed-in-uk-university. [Accessed November 2020].

[93] History.com Editors, "Columbus reaches the "New Word"," HIstory.com, 12 November 2020. [Online]. Available: https://www.history.com/this-day-in-history/columbus-reaches-the-new-world. [Accessed November 2020].

[94] History.com Editors, "U.S. Constitution Signed," 15 September 2020. [Online]. Available: https://www.history.com/this-day-in-history/u-s-constitution-signed. [Accessed November 2020].

[95] Compassion International, "Education Facts," 2020. [Online]. Available: https://www.compassion.com/poverty/education.htm. [Accessed November 2020].

[96] A. Rutherford, "Why racism is not backed by science," The Guardian, 1 March 2015. [Online]. Available: https://www.theguardian.com/science/2015/mar/01/racism-science-human-genomes-darwin. [Accessed November 2020].

[97] National Geographic, "Genetic testing of two European descendants may reveal that they are genetically closer to an African descendant than to each other," August 2019. [Online]. Available: https://www.nationalgeographic.com/culture/2019/07/first-europeans-immigrants-genetic-testing-feature . [Accessed November 2020].

[98] V. B. Ramirez, "World Poverty Has Plummeted—But Will It Ever Disappear?," Singularity University, 2 January 2018. [Online]. Available: https://singularityhub.com/2018/01/02/will-the-world-ever-be-free-of-extreme-poverty/#:~:text=In%201990%20the%20UN%20set,population%20is%20still%20extremely%20poor.. [Accessed November 2020].

[99] Inequality.org, "Income Inequality," 2018. [Online]. Available: https://inequality.org/facts/income-inequality/. [Accessed November 2020].

[100] ZipRecruiter, "Full Time Police Officer Salary," 13 November 2020. [Online]. Available: https://www.ziprecruiter.com/Salaries/Full-Time-Police-Officer-Salary. [Accessed November 2020].

[101] M. Elliott, "How Much Does the Average American Get Paid Per Hour?," Showbiz CheatSheet, 7 September 2018. [Online]. Available: https://www.cheatsheet.com/money-career/how-much-does-the-average-american-get-paid-per-hour.html/. [Accessed November 2020].

[102] E. Martin, "Here's how much the top 5% of Americans make in an hour," Make it, 2 August 2017. [Online]. Available: https://www.cnbc.com/2017/08/02/how-much-the-richest-americans-earn-per-hour.html. [Accessed August 2020].

[103] E. Patten, "Racial, gender wage gaps persist in U.S. despite some progress," Pew Research Center, 1 July 2016. [Online]. [Accessed November 2020].

[104] H. Kharas and a. K. Hamel, "A global tipping point: Half the world is not middle class or wealthier," BROKKINGS, 27 September 2018. [Online]. Available: https://www.brookings.edu/blog/future-development/2018/09/27/a-global-tipping-point-half-the-world-is-now-middle-class-or-wealthier/. [Accessed November 2020].

[105] Lead with Languages, "Top Ten Reasons to Learn Languages," ACTFL, 2020. [Online]. Available: https://www.leadwithlanguages.org/about-us/lead-with-languages/. [Accessed November 2020].

[106] World Population Review, "Literacy Rate by Countries 2020," World Population Review, 2019. [Online]. Available: https://worldpopulationreview.com/country-rankings/literacy-rate-by-country. [Accessed November 2020].

[107] The World Bank, "GDP per capita (current US$)," The World Bank, 2019. [Online]. Available: https://data.worldbank.org/indicator/NY.GDP.PCAP.CD. [Accessed November 2020].

[108] Theirwold, "20 reasons why, in 2020, there are still 260m children out of school," 7 February 2020. [Online]. Available: https://reliefweb.int/report/world/20-reasons-why-2020-there-are-still-260m-children-out-school#:~:text=Theirworld's%20vision%20is%20to%20end,to%20primary%20or%20secondary%20school.. [Accessed November 2020].

[109] World Bank staff, "Population ages 0-14 (% of total population)," The World Bank, 2019. [Online]. Available: https://data.worldbank.org/indicator/SP.POP.0014.TO.ZS. [Accessed November 2020].

[110] KIWISTAT, "Education," 2016. [Online]. Available: https://kiwistat.org/en/education-en/illiterate-worldpopulation/.

# About the Author

Shahid Ahmed grew up in Dhaka and Karachi and worked in Dar-es-Salaam. He has firsthand knowledge of the challenges that perpetuate in slums, chiefly the lack of education. Shahid formed DoPeace in 2014 in the USA and started grassroots campaigns for preschool education in the slums of Bangladesh.

DoPeace began with one school in Rangpur with 22 students. Now there are more than 10,000 students enrolled every year in the DoPeace Learning Centers for the last six years. This rapid growth and successful outcome are due to the extremely low-cost, innovative model that DoPeace pioneered. His endeavor of setting up schools in Bangladesh is chronicled in the book, *Under the Starry Nights: Low-cost Education for Thousands of Children in Slums.*

He has a Ph.D. in Nuclear Engineering from Iowa State University and an MBA from The Wharton School.

He lives in Pennsylvania, the USA, with his wife and enjoys the company of their grandchildren Layla, Ezaan, and Aniya in his free time. You can contact the author at shahid@dopeace.org.

# Index

## E



## F



## G



## H



## I



## J



## L



## M



## N

## O



## P



## R



## S



## T



## U



## W



## Y



## Z

Made in the USA
Monee, IL
04 November 2026

67387548R00154